D1058075

IT'S OK TO TELL

✧ ✧ ✧

IT'S OK TO TELL

A Story of Hope and Recovery

LAUREN BOOK

PROSPECTA PRESS

Published by
Prospecta Press
An imprint of Easton Studio Press
P.O. Box 3131
Westport, CT 06880
(203) 454-4454
www.prospectapress.com

Hardcover ISBN: 978-1935212-43-0
E-book ISBN: 978-1-935212-42-3

First edition

Printed in the United States of America

First printing: February 2011

10 9 8 7 6 5 4 3 2 1

This book is dedicated with love
to Little Lauren and the 39 million
survivors of childhood sexual abuse
in the United States.

*Shed the shame, break the silence,
because it's always ok to tell.*

TABLE OF CONTENTS

Foreword

If you didn't know Lauren Book's story, you might think she had the perfect life. As a child, the eldest daughter of a wealthy Miami lobbyist, Lauren had blond pop star looks, lived in a huge house on the water and had a live-in nanny. But Lauren held a deep, dark secret inside her for most of her childhood. From the time she was thirteen until she was nearly seventeen, someone living inside her home was physically and sexually abusing her. Someone she trusted. Someone she loved.

I met Lauren while shooting a documentary for the Oprah Winfrey Network about sex offenders. Lauren was inside a classroom filled with third graders. She and her partner, Tara, were teaching the kids how to determine when an adult is acting inappropriately. At the time I write this, there are over 700,000 registered sex offenders in the United States, and that number is growing steadily every week.

Lauren had a childlike way about her. She employed a higher-pitched voice when talking to the kids, as though she was one of them. But while she sounded like a kid and even looked liked one, she had a very serious message to get across.

Lauren never told the kids that when she was a little girl her live-in nanny was forcing sex on her. Instead, she and Tara asked the kids to draw pictures of people whom they considered bad or untrustworthy. Not surprisingly, most of the kids drew pictures of men wearing black clothes and masks. Some of them carried big guns and wore mean faces. Almost all of the characters depicted in the kids' pictures were strangers. Lauren told me that kids have been conditioned to think that this is how "bad" people look. They don't look like the people who live inside their homes. They don't look like the people who regularly say "I love you."

Lauren Book's father, Ron, has been a staple of Miami's upper class for as long as she can remember. He drives around in a fancy Audi R8 and is regularly seen in the society photos in the local glossy magazines. Because of how public his life is, the Book family learned to hold things in, to keep private matters private. One of the biggest secrets the family kept was that Lauren's mother had been struggling with depression for years. She had, for all practical purposes, checked out.

So when the Books' live-in nanny started sexually abusing little Lauren, she didn't say anything. Even though she knew what was happening to her was wrong, she didn't want to embarrass the family or allow the lid to come off the sealed container of their home lives. And with a father who was traveling all the time and a near-despondent mother, Lauren's nanny gave the little girl the attention and the affection Lauren thought she needed.

Lauren endured years of physical, sexual, and psychological torture as a child but somehow found the courage to confront her abuser. With the help of her father who stands firmly by his daughter's side, Lauren has become a relentless crusader for kids and women everywhere who have been violated. It's hard enough to hear about the dark place that little Lauren Book inhabited for so many years. I imagine that many people would want to lock the horrifying memories away and move on in silent anonymity. But

Lauren bravely shares her testimony in a very public way so that people will know that the sexual exploitation of a child knows no economic boundaries.

Reading the pages of Lauren's book, your heart will break. You will find yourself utterly shocked and enraged. But you will be inspired by the powerful and courageous voice that has emerged from this young woman who was robbed of her childhood by a sexually violent predator: one of hundreds of thousands out there, many of whom work inside people's homes or places where children congregate.

The world is lucky to have Lauren and her father out there advocating, because neither of them will stop until families are made aware of the dangers that lurk in unexpected places.

Lisa Ling

As the field correspondent for "The Oprah Winfrey Show" and contributor to ABC News' "Nightline" and National Geographic's "Explorer," Lisa Ling has reported from dozens of countries; covering stories about gang rape in the Congo, bride burning in India and the Lord's Resistance Army in Uganda, among other issues that are too often ignored. She is a contributing editor for USA Today's "USA Weekend" magazine. "Our America with Lisa Ling" launched on OWN: the Oprah Winfrey Network in 2011.

1

The Black Swan

November, 2001

It's been three months since I said the words I'd practiced silently for years, so scared of what might happen if I said them out loud.

"My nanny has been forcing me to have sex with her since I was thirteen."

This morning I'm in fifth-period art class, trying to finish the last project for my junior year portfolio, which is due in three days. At school it's easier not to think about everything that's happened since I found the courage to tell. At least here no one knows about it yet. Home is a lot harder. There, it's as if a bomb went off in our house after the truth came out, and it left a crater so deep you can't see the bottom. It feels like maybe I lost an arm and my sister a leg, but we all pretend we can make things normal if we just don't talk about it.

Of course, having the sheriff's deputies around searching for evidence and interviewing each of us one at a time makes that pretty tough. Twice, I've had to go down to the sheriff's station to call Waldy, that's Waldina my abuser, on her cell phone with detectives listening in. They're trying to get her to incriminate herself, but she's too smart for that. My biggest fear, the thing that keeps me up most nights, is the possibility that she'll sneak back to our house to kidnap or hurt me. If she gets her hands on me, I know she'll kill me.

Two weeks after Waldy fled Miami, Dad was already worried that the police were not doing enough to apprehend her. So he hired a private detective who located her in Oklahoma City, and tracked her movements through the months of September and October. All along, Dad relayed whatever information he got to the Broward County sheriff who gave it to the Oklahoma City police. The maddening thing during this time is that everyone knows where Waldy is living; they even know about her new volunteer job coaching ten-year-old girls' soccer. But our sheriff says it's up to his counterpart in Oklahoma City to do the actual apprehension of any suspect dwelling in his city. And for whatever reason, they're not acting.

And this is how it goes from the middle of August to almost the end of November, when I just can't take it anymore. That was three days ago. When I ask Dad for the umpteenth time why they still haven't apprehended her, I'm crying so hard he calls the Broward sheriff while I'm sitting there next to him. I can only hear Dad's side of the conversation.

"Listen, my family is at the end of our rope. If the Oklahoma City sheriff doesn't act in the next forty-eight hours, I'm going to have to take my handgun and drive to Oklahoma City to get the bitch myself . . . . No, I won't calm down. My little girl can't sleep or eat with that woman still out there."

It's true. I'm down to eighty-five pounds.

I go to school the next day, still terrified that Waldy could show up at any time to grab me. But now I have the extra worry that Dad might get in trouble for going to where she is first and shooting her.

At least being in school keeps my mind occupied; it's a lot better than being at home, where all I do is pace and peer out the windows every fifteen minutes. Not that it's easy to study for midterms with all this going on. I've always gotten good grades, but after losing a month and a half of classes while I stayed home, I've fallen behind. With two weeks left before Christmas break, I'm cramming for a physics test and my art portfolio is due this Friday.

I've spent this whole class period trying to figure out how to paint white feathers on my white linen watercolor sheet. The painting is supposed to be of the swans at the pond near our house, and so far I've managed the easy parts: the palm trees at the side of the road, some paddle boats lined up against the shore and even my brother, Chase, and Waldy as little stick figures kicking the soccer ball around in the background. Not that anyone will know it's them.

I look at the clock. There's fifteen minutes left in class, and no more time for do-overs. So I close my eyes and try to imagine the scene again. I'm standing alone by the edge of the water, watching the swans glide across the pond like ballerinas in a perfect line. The swan in front points her head straight up and takes off, leaving a wake of ripples, making the others bob on the water behind her. What I want to paint is what comes next, when there's nothing but air above and below her. Our swans never fly far or stay up in the air for very long. They just want a break. God, me too!

I can do this, I tell myself. I pick up the smallest, thinnest brush, dip it in black, and paint the outline of the swan's head and wingspan just after she spreads her wings. *Nice . . . now if I can fill in the sky behind her without messing—Oh darn . . . just what I was afraid of . . .* the black paint is running down my sheet, covering the swan like the sky is raining tar.

I put my head down on my knees.

"Is something wrong, Lauren?" It's my art teacher.

"I ruined it."

She's looking at my painting, twisting her mouth. "Maybe not. Do you know about black swans?"

"I thought they only came in white."

"The first black swans were discovered in Australia in the sixteenth century. They were so rare they became a symbol for things that are unusual and unexpected."

"So, you think I should make it black?"

"You're already halfway there," she says with a smile. "Their beaks are fire engine red, not orange like the ones on other swans and geese," she adds before moving on to the next easel.

I dip a big fat brush into the black paint, relieved that I might be able to salvage my painting and my art grade today. In my mind's eye, a mysterious new swan appears at our pond; its midnight-colored feathers drawing everyone's attention as it lifts off. I cover my bird's body in black. I'm just about to add a touch of red to his beak when I hear my name again.

"Lauren . . ." This time it's the school nurse poking her head in the door. "Come here, please." She says it in a dramatic whisper and then steps back to wait in the hall. I have a sinking feeling in my stomach as I put my brush down on the palette and get up.

"Your father just called. You need to pick up Chase and go home right away."

At least that means Dad is all right. "Why?" I ask the nurse.

"He didn't say. Just that it's urgent."

"Okay." I look back at my painting, feeling torn, wanting to finish the sky around my swan and be done with it, but knowing I have to get home ASAP. Something must have happened. I look at my watch. It's twelve-fifty.

I pick up Chase, who's waiting for me outside the lower school. He gets in the car and doesn't even ask why we're leaving early. Maybe it's because every day since August 15, the day I told, has been different, and usually not in a good way. Even with all the bad things Waldy did to me, she brought stability to my life. And now that's gone. It may seem odd for me to say that sometimes I miss my abuser, but I wouldn't be honest if I didn't admit it. It doesn't help that the whole world has gone crazy. Right after I told and Waldy took off, we had 9/11, and then anthrax killed two people in Boca Raton. Now everyone is just as petrified as me. Could someone just please stop this scary ride? I really, really want to get off.

We make it home in ten minutes.

"No offense, but I'm not eating the lunch you made me this morning," Chase says as he tosses his brown lunch bag into the trash like he's shooting a three-pointer. "Can I put a frozen pizza in the microwave?"

"Whatever," I say as I hurry into the living room where Mom is sitting on the sofa with the television blasting. "What's going on?" I ask.

Mom turns toward me and shakes her head. Her eyes are red, but it's probably because she's still up from last night. She doesn't say anything, but then she doesn't have to. The newswoman on TV is saying it all.

"Waldina Flores, the former nanny for the children of top Florida lawyer, lobbyist and power broker Ron Book has been arrested in Oklahoma City. Broward County detectives brought Flores back to

Fort Lauderdale today to face charges for the sexual abuse of Ron Book's eldest daughter, which it is alleged went on for four years in the accuser's home."

There's Waldy's mug shot on television. She looks mad. It's the same glare I'd get whenever I'd say no to her; a look I always thought she saved for me, part of the arsenal of tricks she used to terrorize and control me. Now it feels like she's sending me a message that I'd better look out, she's back in Fort Lauderdale and she's gonna get me. My stomach does a flip as I watch.

Video of our neighborhood plays on the screen while a reporter gives more details about the charges and our family. Now there's blood rushing to my head, making me dizzy, like it did when Waldy would grab me, digging her nails into my arm, before she whacked me with a hairbrush, or dug her car keys into my side, causing a sharp pain like the one that's shooting up and down me right now.

My next thought is for my little brother. He can't see this.

"Turn it off, before Chase—"

"Hey, a truck with a satellite dish just drove real slow by our house. It says Channel 7 on the roof." It's Chase yelling from the foyer. "I'm going outside to see."

"Don't open the door!" I scream.

By then Chase, Mom and I are in the foyer and the front door is cracked open.

"Get off my street before I call the sheriff!" That's Dad yelling at the reporters as he slams the door behind himself. Then, talking into a cell phone: "Yeah, it's an emergency. I've got trespassers pointing cameras at my house and children. This is a private, gated community. They shouldn't even be in here. There's even a couple of helicopters circling around over my house. The address is 10711 Hawks Vista Street in Plantation and you better get out here, pronto."

He looks at us and says, "Lauren, take Chase upstairs and both of you get started on homework."

Right. Like that's even possible, I think but don't say.

"You heard me," he says. "Where's Samantha?"

"She's still on her class trip," I remind him. "They're not coming back until Thursday."

"Oh, right," he says.

I take Chase by the elbow.

"Leave your TVs off," Dad says as he turns toward his study.

Mom follows him, asking, "Why do they have to say it's your 'eldest daughter?' I thought there was a law about that."

"Damn it. Do you think I wanted her name out there?"

From the living room, the TV newscasters have finished with us and they're going on about clear skies and cooling temperatures.

"What happened?" Chase asks me when we get to his room and I sit down on the bed. "Did they catch Waldy?"

"Yeah."

"Where is she?"

"In the Broward County jail."

"So, do you think we can visit her there?"

"Shhhh," I say with a finger to my lips. "Dad will go nuts if he hears that."

Even though it's been explained to him several times, eleven-year-old Chase still looks confused. Then it occurs to me . . . *I was just a year older than he is now when Waldy came to our house and started abusing me.*

April, 2002

It's five months later, and I'm in a hot, stuffy room at the Broward County courthouse being deposed, meaning questioned by lawyers under oath about how the abuse started. It's bad enough that I have to do this, but I'm doubly uncomfortable wearing a black dress with pantyhose and low heels. I really miss my jeans, but Mom and Dad decided this outfit makes me look innocent or pure, or whatever it is I'm supposed to look like so nobody will think I deserved what happened to me. As if to prove their point, Waldy's public defender, who already has the information that I was twelve when Waldy first came to our house, begins the deposition sounding as if he doesn't know who started the sex between us and which one of us wanted to keep it going. Sometimes it really does feel like I'm the one on trial.

The man asking questions is the public defender. I'm the one giving the short answers.

> Q. *Was there some of the sexual activity that was allegedly engaged in Plantation initiated by you?*
>
> A. *No.*
>
> Q. *—or consensually—*
>
> A. *No.*
>
> Q. *—engaged in—*
>
> A. *No.*

After that doesn't work, he tries to trip me up on the numbers. Like I counted. Don't people realize when you're being raped in your own house, all you can think about is surviving that minute, or the night? And when you wake up it's all about getting through the day.

Q. How many times in Plantation, to the best of your knowledge?

A. I can't say. It had to depend on who was in the house, how much time there was. It depended.

Q. Okay. Can you . . . give me some kind of estimate, like more than five, more than ten?

A. It was definitely more than ten.

Q. Maybe ten, maybe more?

A. More

Q. Fifteen?

A. More.

Q. Okay. Twenty?

A. More probably.

By the time I'm giving this deposition, Waldy has been in jail for four months and her trial date is still several more months away. Because each step of the legal process is covered in the media, Waldy's face and the words "Ron Book's eldest daughter" are in the news, regularly. During it all, I've been asked hundreds of times by the state's attorney, my parents, kids at school and anyone else who recognizes me why I didn't say something sooner. I hope by the time I finish telling my story you'll understand why.

Another question I hear a lot (or I know people would like to ask) is how does a girl get sexually abused by a woman. They assume it's always a male abuser. Although it usually is, there's a lot more abuse of girls (and boys) by females than anyone talks about. Not that I relish being the one to break the silence on that really uncomfortable issue. But I guess I have to.

The other thing people want to know is where my parents were while all this abuse was going on. I'll do my best to answer that honestly, too. As a family, we had problems before Waldy became our nanny. Out of respect for my mother's privacy, I will not discuss the exact nature of her emotional issues. I wish I didn't have to reveal anything about it. In the spirit of accuracy and compassion, I know she always wanted the best for me and loves me. In order for you to understand how the abuse I describe could have taken place in our household, and why it went on for so long, you need to understand the void created by my mother's terrible emotional issues and her involuntary shortcomings as a parent. Throughout my story, I depict these realities only from my own perspective as a child, and then as a teenager. Unfortunately, these problems, you could call them our family dysfunctions, gave a sexual predator like Waldy an opening that she then exploited for her own ends.

Sometimes, those four years when I was being abused are a blur to me; or like it's someone else's life I'm talking about. Mandy Wells, my counselor from the Broward County Sexual Assault Treatment Center, calls that disassociating. Kids who are sexually violated split off from themselves in order to get through the experience. But once you're safe, she says, it's important to let the memories come back. That's one of the reasons why I'm going to start from the beginning. You need to have all the information if you're going to understand any of this. And so I'm including the court documents as well as giving you my own memory of the events.

In my deposition, the public defender asks me about when Waldy first came to our house.

> Q. *Waldina was hired by your parents. And were you told by your mom and dad that you have to do what Waldina says?*
>
> A. *She was in charge and we had respect for whoever came into the house and she was in charge. That was how it was.*

*Q. Did you view her as an interloper in your life—another
wanna be parent?*

*A. Once I let her into my life, yes, I did view her as another
parent.*

Waldy *was* like a parent to me—a very bad and selfish parent.
But it was a whole lot more complicated than that. Like I said, I'm
going to tell the whole story as honestly as I can, from day one.

2

Mothers, Surrogates and Daughters

August, 1997

"You're twelve years old and you're sure you don't need a nanny, which is probably the best reason for you to have one," Dad says to me while I stand in the doorway to his and Mom's bathroom. He's at the sink with an electric razor humming in one hand and a cell phone in the other, checking his messages. Today is the first day of school for me.

"But I'll be thirteen in five weeks."

"Have you eaten your breakfast?"

"I've been doing my hair." I slide my hand from my bangs to the ponytail to make sure no strands wandered loose in the last five minutes.

He winks. "Go eat."

I stay where I am.

"Don't forget your mother is going to be extra busy with her new store from now on."

"So? Like that changes anything," I say, thinking about Mom still asleep in their adjoining bedroom.

"Hey, pipsqueak, give Dad a break. I want you to help Waldina get settled."

"Waldina? What kind of name is that?" I ask in my brattiest tone.

He lifts his eyebrows in warning. "She's from Honduras. Her English is very good. We're lucky to get her on such short notice after Lindy upped and quit without warning."

"I actually liked Lindy. Mom made sure she didn't stay long."

"All the more reason to help your new nanny get off to a good start." He checks his wristwatch and pushes a button on his phone before putting it down on the counter. It rings once, and then a female voice comes on speaker. "Good morning, Ron. How are you today?"

"Terrific," Dad says as he keeps shaving. "Listen, Janet, who's my first meeting?"

To me he says, "Make sure Chase eats a bowl of cereal, not some junk food. I'm dropping the three of you off at school on my way in."

Janet's voice: "It's a partners' monthly meeting."

"Okay. Tell them I'll be no more than ten minutes late. What about after that?"

"Two gentlemen from the RPOF," Janet says.

As Dad listens and shaves, I think about asking him for a carpool to get us back and forth from school until I'm old enough to drive. But I don't get that far.

"Got it. One more thing, Janet. Please call my insurance guy and have him put the new nanny on my auto policy. It's Waldina Flores. Right, Wal-dee-na with a 'W' . . . Of course she has a driver's license and a Social Security number. Just let him know that'll be coming."

"But Dad—"

He gives me an impatient look that signals that it's time for me to leave.

I really don't think we need another nanny. It's not that I love having so much work to do around the house. I'm just used to doing it. And I've gotten to where I think it's easier to keep it that way, instead of stopping every time we have a new nanny then starting again when they leave. Our routine is usually that on Sundays Dad and I go grocery shopping, and then I cook dinners when Mom's not up to it. I get Chase ready for school in the morning, and I make sure he has a bath before bedtime. Of course, I take care of myself, and Sam pretty much does her own thing. It's been this way for years.

Our nannies usually quit because Mom can be pretty difficult to please. Or she fires them for reasons that only she understands. When she's on one of her tangents, she stays up all night and then sleeps until two or three in the afternoon. Mom has her sweet moments, too, but we've learned not to trust them too much. It's like a switch flips; and all of a sudden she'll turn on you, yelling and sometimes throwing things. Her fury is not usually directed at me; it's more between her and Sam. The two of them have never gotten along. I'm the Goody two-shoes. But Sam, who's two years younger than me, doesn't take crap from anyone. That's why she and Mom fight so much.

Chase, who's seven this year, is everyone's golden boy. He has blond hair and green eyes like mine (and Mom's), and he's really cute and funny. He's also learned to stay out of the way when Mom goes off on Sam, or when Mom's arguing with Dad. They fight a lot at night in their bedroom, which shares a wall with Chase's room. When it started getting loud and keeping him awake, Chase began asking me to hang out with him, reading or rubbing his back until he fell asleep. Now I sleep there most nights in his double bed. It's just easier that way.

"What would you like the children to call you?" Mom asks later that day as the three of us are standing in the kitchen being introduced to our new nanny.

I can't believe she just called me a child. I'm so embarrassed.

At Mom's question, Waldina looks up from chopping onions and shines a big-toothed smile at us. "You can all call me Waldy," she says.

"Hi, Waldy," says Sam, barely looking in her direction before she's out of the room.

One second later, Chase is standing next to her at the counter. "Nice to meet you, Waldy. What are you making for dinner?"

"How would you like tacos?" she asks.

"I like them, a lot," he answers. "Can I chop something?"

Waldy hands him some cheese and a grater, and while she's showing him how to use it, I have time to size her up. She's got to be at least thirty years old. It's hard to tell with people as big as Waldy. She's short, too; maybe five foot three, I guess, since I'm barely five feet. She's wearing dark drawstring shorts with sandals and a sleeveless white blouse. *I sure wouldn't want her picking out my clothes,* I think but keep to myself.

When I look over at Mom she's glaring at me; I guess I'm supposed to be cheery and welcoming. I shrug. She shakes her head in disgust and walks over to the stool next to Chase where she's laid her purse. From a front pocket she digs out her car keys and glasses case. "I'm sorry but I really need to go. I have somebody coming in to help with the window display at four-thirty." Then, wearing her dark sunglasses with the lime green rims, she closes the latch on her purse. "Oh, I've thought of the perfect name for the store."

We wait through Mom's dramatic pause to hear her official pronouncement of the name that we know she's been working on for weeks.

"I'll call it Confection Connection."

"What's that mean?" asks Chase, staring at her blankly.

"A confection is a handmade sweet thing, like a chocolate drop, a cake or a cookie. It's the perfect name because we'll bake everything right in the store, with each item custom ordered."

"Wow," says Chase with a big smile on his face.

I have a hard time imagining Mom organizing all that, let alone doing any of it for more than a day. But then I always get a little nervous when she's this up about anything, since a crash is usually not far behind.

"I like that name," I say, hoping for a way out of the immediate situation. "Can I come with you?"

"Not tonight. I'll be there very late. And I'm counting on you to help Waldy until she knows her way around the house." To Waldy she says, "Just ask Lauren if you need anything. Bye now."

I sigh, dreading the long evening until Dad gets home from work.

"Chase, if you want to swim, I'm going in now," I say, picking up my backpack. I avoid Waldy's gaze as I leave the kitchen.

A month and a half later, I'm walking with Sam, Chase and Waldy the three blocks from our house to the community park. During this time with Waldy as our new nanny, I've been keeping my distance from her; sometimes throwing in some hostility to make sure she knows I don't need or want her around.

"Why are you so mean to her?" Samantha asks me.

Chase, holding the soccer ball, is walking up ahead with Waldy while Sam and I bring up the rear.

"You made her cry."

"If she can't handle a little sass, tough luck," I answer, though I'm feeling a bit guilty about telling Waldy to "butt out and leave me alone" when all she'd done was offer to make my lunch. And I'd seen her tears, too, before she'd wiped them away with a dish towel.

"If you keep it up, she's going to leave, and then you know . . .?"

I understand what Sam's getting at, but I'm not so sure the "you know" is any worse than having Waldy boss me around like she's the new mom at our house. It's been a month and a half, and though I have to admit things are running pretty smoothly, I'm not comfortable with her yet. Like I told my friend Stacey, sometimes I wish I'd break my leg so I could be the center of attention for a day, and I don't mean the nanny's attention. Stacey said she knew just what I meant.

When we get to the field, Waldy starts kicking the ball back and forth in a triangle with Chase and Sam. "Lauren, come play with us," she yells to me as I sit down cross-legged on the grass.

"I don't feel like it," I yell back.

"What's the matter?" she asks in a teasing voice as she walks toward me. "Aren't you any good?"

"I'm good, and I'm fast. But what if I break my leg out there?" I ask, thinking maybe this is the time to try my idea for getting Mom and Dad's attention.

"Why would you worry about that, Lauren?"

"Let's just say . . ."

"It sounds like you want to break your leg. Okay, then I'll help you do it." She says it like it's a dare.

I know what you're thinking. The broken leg thing was a pathetic, childish ploy. I hate to admit I was so desperate for love that I'd even think of it, but I was and I did. It's hard for me to really get across how lonely I was back then. Even now, I'm ashamed that I ever felt that needy when there are so many kids in the world who have it a lot worse. Here I was, this lucky girl who grew up with every material thing anyone could ever want. I understood that, and I certainly put up a good front: the perfect daughter, an A student and the responsible older sister. But inside, I was like one of those orphan babies you see on TV who get a bed to sleep in and food to eat, but they have no one to hold them or love them. So they just wither away and don't even cry anymore. It seems ludicrous to compare myself to an impoverished orphan, but when I saw those sad little babies' faces on TV, I felt as though I knew exactly what they were feeling. Today I realize that loneliness is an equal opportunity emotion. It's also an open door for someone who is a sexual predator of children.

So there I am feeling dejected while sitting on the edge of the soccer field with Waldy towering over me. At this point, I really don't want her to think I'm serious about breaking any of my body parts for any reason, so I get up.

"Never mind," I say as I run past her onto the field.

I guess you could say it's around this time when I cave and let go of my "I don't need anybody" act.

After that, on most days Waldy wakes us up, takes us to school and picks us up in the afternoons. Most evenings, she cooks dinner and cleans up the dishes. She even wakes me up in the morning, then helps me pick out my clothes and get dressed. *Maybe she'll stay,* I think. *Maybe everything is going to be easier now. Maybe I'll get to be a kid after all.*

It's called "grooming." That's the word used by those of us who are trying to alert people to the tricks child predators employ to lure children into their control, and it's what Waldy was doing with me during these first few months she lived and worked in our home. It's an important danger sign for parents who employ nannies or other caregivers to watch their children. After a pedophile or sexual predator selects his or her next victim, he or she grooms that child into being perfect, docile prey. The predator does it by giving treats and special attention that appeal to any child, but especially to one who is lonely, neglected or simply shy, and who, with busy, working parents, doesn't usually receive that kind of attention.

Since 90 percent of sexual abuse is committed by an adult in the child's inner circle—a parent, older sibling or cousin; a coach, babysitter or neighbor—the abuser has many opportunities to groom his or her victim. In my case, Waldy let me stay up late, much later than Sam or Chase. She invited me to watch TV in her private quarters. She bribed me with special foods. She constantly told me how pretty I was, and how much *she* appreciated me, even if no one else in the family did. Her predatory actions went under my parents' radar simply because it looked like the behavior of a doting nanny, and because they, like most parents, didn't have a clue what to look for.

December, 1997

The Confection Connection is a huge success. Orders are piling in. At first they're mostly Dad's clients, but after Thanksgiving lots of other people are calling and coming in, too. The store is right on Biscayne Boulevard, close to the Aventura Mall, which is mobbed at this time of year. Mom hired two ladies to work the counter and the phone, taking and filling orders. But it's gotten so busy with Hanukah and Christmas coming, she's brought Waldy in to help during the day. After school and on weekends, I go, too. Sometimes we work until midnight or one in the morning, and I love it, especially making the candy. I make sure each piece is perfect, or it goes into the "No" pile. Mom says I have to stop eating my failures or I'll become a blimp by the New Year.

One Friday night Mom and the others have gone home, leaving Waldy and me to handle customers until eight o'clock closing time. Waldy's mixing chocolate in the kitchen while I help a customer out front.

I recognize the guy I'm waiting on; he works at Power Smoothie in the mall. I like to tease boys buying chocolates, because they're so easily embarrassed. This one picks out a half-dozen hearts, which I put in a little pink box.

"That's $3.50. Are they for your girlfriend or your mom?"

"Ah, neither . . . I just like 'em . . . especially the pistachio creams."

He hands me a five-dollar bill.

"Cool, because I made those myself this morning," As I open the money drawer, I pop the big gum bubble I've just blown. He cracks a smile, then takes a chocolate heart out of the box and puts it in his mouth.

"Wow, you make these?" he asks, smacking his lips.

I nod and, with my gum snapping loudly, hand over the change.

"I'll be back," he says.

When the door shuts behind him, I turn to see Waldy watching me from the door to the kitchen.

"Take that gum out of your mouth," she says, frowning.

"Why? It's not bothering anyone."

"It's not ladylike."

I shrug. "You can't make me."

Her frown gets deeper and she tilts her head, as if she's considering her options. "I can and I will," she says.

The next thing I know, she's got her hands behind my head and her lips are fastened on mine. Then she pushes her tongue into my mouth and uses it to grab the gum and pull it out of my mouth and into hers. Our "kiss" lasts no more than ten seconds, but before she even takes her mouth away from mine, I've left my body. Looking down from the ceiling, I watch this strange scene while the rest of me is in free fall. When Waldy finally releases me and puts some space between us, it's like I've landed on the tile floor with a painful thud, even though I'm standing in the same place. What just happened? I have no idea. My eyes have still not adjusted to being back in my head. I put my shaking hands in my apron pockets and turn to face the front of the store, where the hearts display is a glittering blur against the headlights on Biscayne Boulevard. As I wipe her saliva off my lips, I'm relieved to hear Waldy's footsteps walking away, then the ping of my gum landing in the trash can and the kitchen doors swinging closed.

I avoid Waldy for the next two days, telling Mom I have to

study for finals, so I can't come to the store. When I'm home, I make sure Waldy and I are never alone in the same room. But then school vacation starts, and Mom asks me to come back to the store. "All hands on deck or forget Christmas presents this year," she says, giving me no choice. And after the first couple of days, with three or four of us always there and the constant rush of customers, I start to relax and almost forget what happened.

Until one morning, when I'm alone in the kitchen pouring white chocolate into molds at the prep table and I hear Waldy's heavy footsteps behind me. On the table is a hot vat of chocolate, with spoons and scoopers for mixing and plastic guns of different sizes for squeezing out the fillings. I've almost finished pouring chocolate into a tray of swans, when she speaks.

"Hey, we should talk. I can tell you're upset."

I act as if I don't hear her and keep working, carefully removing the mold to reveal the finished white swans.

"Lauren," she repeats.

"I don't want to talk about it," I tell her without turning around. When she moves next to me, I drop my hands to the table and stare straight ahead, scanning the racks of molds. Only my eyes are moving. On the bottom row there are geometric and celestial shapes: cubes, domes, triangles, suns, stars and halfmoons. Then come the barnyard animals: horses, pigs and lambs. Next we have our specialty car molds; the most popular models are the Mustang convertible and a Jag, which we do in different colors.

Finally, I return my eyes to the sheet of swans now cooling on a finishing tray. I admire the arc of their necks, and check for any deformities.

"Really, I'm too busy right now," I say to Waldy, who's still standing next to me.

"You can stop for one minute to talk to me." She puts a hand on my forearm, which makes me go rigid. "You're mistaken if you think what I did was wrong. Kisses are what people give someone they love."

She loves me? I'm still staring at the tray of swans, wondering if what she's saying can be true.

"Like that?" I ask, remembering her tongue in my mouth.

"Yeah, except without the gum."

"Oh." I finally do a half-turn to look at her.

She makes her face all soft. I swear her eyes are tearing. "I care about you, you silly thing. I would never do anything to hurt you."

"Oh . . ." Now I feel guilty for the way I've acted toward her since it happened. "No one ever did that to me before. I'm really . . . sorry."

She slides up closer and puts her hand on my cheek, then kisses my forehead lightly. As she plays with my ponytail with her free hand, she keeps talking in a monotone. "I understand. You've just never been kissed right before. It's okay. I forgive you. You're so pretty. It's about time someone appreciated you."

On her face was the closed-mouth smile I would come to know all too well before this was over. At the time, I took it to mean just what she'd said. That she cared about me. And she thought I was pretty, even if no one else did. Now, however, I see it as the sly, guarded expression of a predatory cat stalking her prey: me, the clueless mouse-girl she was setting up for the pounce. By this point, I had been perfectly "groomed" for Waldy's first sexual advance. The kiss was a test on her part, but it wasn't even a particularly risky one. If I complained to anyone, she could deny that it was anything inappropriate. And just say she was reprimanding me for being unladylike.

"I have to finish these before the chocolate cools," I say, still feeling nervous and confused by what I'm hearing from her. I need to be alone to think.

"Sure, go ahead." Her eyes light up as she smiles again, releasing my hand slowly but with her fingers still stroking mine.

She goes back out front, leaving me in a daze. It's weird. I'm warm all over, and it's hard to breathe. I feel as if I've just done five laps around the track. I lean over the prep table and take as much air into my lungs as I can, and exhale for as long as I can; then I do it again. It's like I've just joined a secret club where people are incredibly affectionate and go around kissing on the lips and saying they love each other out loud. In fourth and fifth grade, I had a "boyfriend" named Timmy. But all we ever did was exchange notes and sit together at lunch and maybe hold hands. I don't know all the rules to this new club yet, but I have to admit it doesn't feel all bad. So maybe it's okay. I mean, it's just kissing and touching and saying sweet things. But if it's not naughty, why do I feel I have to keep it secret? I don't know, and I can't think of who to ask.

In my mind, I try to sort out this kissing thing. Sure, I've thought about being kissed. Stacey and I practiced on a mirror once, imagining it was Ricky Martin's face we were smooching. But then we started laughing so hard we fell off the bed.

Waldy loves me? How weird that she said that.

I know my dad loves me. But this is different.

Maybe because it's been so long since my mother kissed or hugged me, or told me that she loved me, I've literally lost track of what I might be missing. But wait a minute . . . I *know* the way Waldy kissed me the other night is *not* how I've seen other mothers kiss their daughters. *So what is this?*

3

Firsts

Do you remember your first school dance? The memories I have of mine are supersized because I'd only recently turned thirteen, and it was my first social event as a teenager. Plus there was the fact that this Valentine's Day dance simultaneously marked the beginning and end of my life as a typical teen; one big exciting week of "normal" before everything went awry.

On the Sunday before the big dance, my going was only a 90 percent done deal. I was still waiting on Dad's final decision about whether I could go. For a while, it didn't look good. He kept putting off the conversation, and now Florida's legislative session, which goes from March to May every year, was about to start. This mattered in our family because, before and during the session, Dad would spend Monday through Friday in Tallahassee lobbying for his clients. He was leaving tonight for the week, so I was running out of time to get him to say yes.

It's time for our regular Sunday kickball game, Dad's way of making sure we have some quality family time during this hectic season. Now that Waldy is living with us, she usually plays too, especially now that she no longer takes Sunday or any other day off. The fact that she's there every day I view as a good thing; I'd much rather have her around acting as a buffer against my mother's bad moods than have to deal with Mom myself, especially now that Mom is getting on Sam's case more often.

Chase, Sam, Waldy and I are with Dad out on the street in front of the house, arranged in a diamond to kick and field the ball. Mom sits on the grass watching. This time, Dad and I are on one team, so I have his ear and can make my case about the dance.

"Please, Daddy, everyone is going."

"Pipsqueak, I don't know. You've got older kids there who may have God knows what in their pockets."

While Dad is talking, Waldy moves closer to us, clearly listening.

"Mr. Ron, I can take her into the gym and wait right outside after it's over."

Dad looks at Waldy and then at me. I can tell he's reconsidering.

"Please, Daddy."

A pause, then, "All right, all right, but don't leave the gym until you see Waldy."

"Thank you. Thank you." I hug him tight around the waist.

The next day after school, Mom and I go shopping to buy me a dress to wear to the dance. Although when we were younger, Mom and Dad used to dress me and Sam up in matching outfits, it's not something we do anymore since our school requires uniforms. Now it's khaki slacks or shorts with a short-sleeved crew shirt on school days. Around the house, I'm in jeans or shorts or my bathing suit.

So this is probably the first time in years I've asked for a dress.

Mom picks me up after school, and we go straight to the mall. After an hour, we've already blown through Bloomingdale's and Nordstrom's, and we've made it to Macy's junior department. Britney Spears's "Baby One More Time" is playing loudly through speakers hanging right above our heads. I suppose it's to let teens know this is *our place,* and keep everyone else out—except mothers with credit cards, of course.

"How about this?" I ask, holding up a navy denim empire-waist mini.

Frowning, Mom says, "With our coloring we really have to stay away from those dark shades." She runs a hand through her platinum blond spikes before turning back to the dresses.

"Oh, okay." I'd never considered the concept of matching my skin and hair with my clothes. I try to picture what that other blond, fair-skinned teen—the famous one, Britney Spears—would have worn to her first school dance. Unfortunately, what comes to mind is Britney in one of the hooker outfits she favors for her live shows. The only pictures I've seen of her are the ones that make Mom and Dad vow I'll never get their permission to go to one of her concerts, not that I've ever asked.

"Here, try these on," Mom says, handing me an armful of the dresses she's picked out.

"Okay," I say, relieved to be spared any further searching.

A half hour later, after trying on eight dresses without a clear winner, I've come back to the one I liked a little bit the first time around. It's a mini with a snug pink top and a frilly white petticoat skirt. As I do a twirl for the wraparound fitting room mirror, I get a kick out of how the skirt balloons out in layers like a soft ice cream cone, and how it bounces when I move.

Mom, sitting on a chair opposite me, shakes her head. "It makes you look fat," she says, scrunching her nose.

Usually, I look as skinny as a cardboard cutout. At least in this, I almost have boobs and hips. I watch and wait for Mom's final answer, as she gets up and steps in front of me to check out her profile in the mirror.

"Let's forget it," I say, just wanting to be out of there.

"No, no, get it if you want it," she answers, turning from the mirror and grabbing her purse. "We've still got to find you some heels."

Wow, another first, I think, perking up. "Pink ones?"

"Pink or white will do, but they can't be more than an inch high or your father will explode."

"Or I'll fall on my face." I put my new dress back on its hanger and hand it to Mom. As I pull my khakis and yellow crew shirt back on, I'm excited again; also relieved to think that I'll have four-and-a-half days to practice walking around in my one-inch high-heeled shoes before Saturday night.

On Saturday afternoon, I'm counting the minutes until it's time to start getting ready. For dinner, I get down a few forkfuls of spaghetti, enough to satisfy Dad that I won't faint. After my shower, Waldy dries and brushes out my hair, and then Mom comes in and applies rouge, lipstick, eye liner and shadow, more firsts for me. Then I finally get to put on my new dress and heels. When I'm ready, Chase and Sam, who are watching and getting excited, go down the hall to cue Dad, who gets the video camera going and records my entrance. On tape, the look on my face matches my memory of that moment perfectly: I feel like a princess, and I haven't even left the house yet.

By the time I get to the dance, my excitement is still there, but matched by a feeling of sheer terror.

"Do you want me to walk you in?" Waldy asks, as she drives past the drop-off point and into the parking lot outside the middle school.

"I guess."

We get to outside the gymnasium, and I hear the loud music. Inside, I see red and blue beams of light crisscrossing the basketball court, where hundreds of Valentine hearts are hanging from the ceiling. I stand back to allow a bunch of kids I recognize as eighth graders in through the double doors.

"I don't see anybody I know," I say. Actually, since our private school isn't that big, I see mostly familiar faces but none from the small circle of kids I call my friends.

Waldy pulls me away from the door and takes my hand. "Here's what we'll do. I'll go sit in the car. If, by eight o'clock, a half-hour from now, you don't want to stay, just call me and I'll come back to this spot and we can go home."

"Okay," I say, opening my little purse to make sure my cell phone is in there and charged.

"Lauren!"

I look up to see Stacey trotting out of the gym toward me.

"This is so cool," she yells. "There's a light show and a DJ. Come on . . . what are you waiting for? Let's go."

"I'm coming."

"You'll be the prettiest girl in there," Waldy whispers in my ear before she releases my hand.

A few minutes later, Stacey and I are dancing to Spice Girls, Boyz II Men and Ricky Martin. For fast songs, it doesn't matter who you're dancing with. But when a slow one comes on and everyone starts hooking up into pairs, Stacey and I escape to the refreshment table. After a couple of minutes, we're part of a bunch of kids from our seventh-grade class. There's a lot of goofing around and flirting going on, which means poking, teasing and laughing uproariously when the person you fancy says something even a tiny bit funny. I haven't singled out any one boy. I'm happy just to be out of the house and there with my friends.

A bit later, I'm standing on the edge of the dance floor, studying the moves of the coolest dancers, when Stacey leaves the crowd by the refreshment table and grabs my elbow. "Come with me," she says. I follow her to the girls' room and into one of the stalls, where she makes an important announcement.

"Scott likes you," she tells me in a theatrical whisper.

"No he doesn't."

"Uh-huh," she says teasingly.

"How do you know?"

"Because he told Tommy, who told Chelsea, who told Brandon, who just told me."

"Oh," I respond, taking the comment more seriously given the pedigree of the messengers involved—all members of the seventh-grade "in crowd."

"Besides, you can tell by the way he acts so dorky around you," Stacey explains in an authoritative tone.

"That's true," I answer, thinking about how the tall and gangly Scott had spilled soda on the front of his shirt when I told him that I liked his Mickey Mouse tie.

This would be enough to make my night, but it gets even better.

Back by the refreshment table, I flash a big smile at Scott, who's morphed into a more confident version of himself, probably because he knows what Stacey just told me and has seen my positive response.

"Wanna dance?" he asks.

"Sure."

As luck would have it, it's a slow song. I stand there, not knowing what to do next, as Scott takes my hand and leads me out to the center of the gym. Once we're facing each other, he steps closer and puts his palms on the small of my back. I can't reach his shoulders, so I put my hands on his upper arms, and off we go. I like the way we sway and rock together, and the little charges that go off inside me when we brush up against each other. Stacey, dancing with Brandon not far from us, flashes me a thumbs-up sign.

When the song ends, shy Scott returns. He can barely look at me, and he's completely speechless. Feeling emboldened, I yank gently on his tie and say, "I'll see you at lunch on Monday," code for "let's sit together and be a 'couple.'"

"Yeah, sure," he says, his freckled face now beaming, setting off his heavily-gelled orange-red hair.

Next there's a raffle prize drawing and a dance contest, which I sit out on the bleachers with Scott and Stacey and Brandon. Then the big clock above the basketball net hits nine-thirty, and the DJ wraps for the night.

I hadn't thought about Waldy once after I walked into the gym. As I exit with my little group, I'm embarrassed to find her waiting for me in the same spot, as planned.

"See you guys," I say to Stacey, Scott and Brandon. I slink away as they continue walking.

After giving Waldy a quick hello, I crouch down and pretend to be fixing the strap on my shoe long enough for my friends to reach the far end of the sidewalk. I really don't want to run into them again on our way to the car.

"Did you have a good time?" Waldy asks casually.

"Yes, it was great."

I'm relieved that she doesn't ask for details.

Not so for Mom and Dad, who want more than a headline. So I give my sixty-second report: Yes, I danced. Yes, with a boy. And, yes, I had major fun. Relief is painted all over their faces. After that, I run upstairs to tell Sam, who pouted all afternoon about the fact that she, being in fifth grade, wasn't old enough to go. We hang out and watch TV for a while, and then I end up sleeping in the bedroom she and I share.

The next day, Sunday, Stacey and I spend hours on the phone, dissecting and reliving the highlights of the night, which you pretty much just read about in their totality. During my bath Sunday night, I'm already rehearsing what I'll say to Scott the next day at lunch. In the peculiar logic of first crushes, I can't decide whether I like him yet, but I'm happy he's decided to like me. After getting into my nightgown, I go back to Chase's room to sleep. He's waiting for me, and he's got a book picked out for me to read aloud.

For a bunch of reasons, I want to pause here, at least to take a few breaths. The truth is, I dread telling what happens next. Even though I've done it in hundreds of talks with other abuse survivors, counselors and, of course, the police and the state's attorney, it's never easy; especially this time when I've been remembering all the fun that came right before it. If I stop right here, you could go away with the impression that I had an okay childhood in a pretty dysfunctional family. But I can't stop, because my story is supposed to help people understand how abuse can happen to anyone, even people with enough money to afford a nanny. Beyond that, I want you to understand that it happens more often to kids like me, who at that point in my life felt very alone and abandoned.

Here's how, during my deposition, the public defender gets into what happened next. This is after I told him about that night in Confection Connection, when Waldy kissed me.

> *Q: Were you frightened of this act that Waldina allegedly performed?*
>
> *A: I was frightened because I knew that it was abnormal.*

Which was true, but there's a lot that I couldn't say because, just like when you're on the stand in court, you only answer questions; you are not supposed to volunteer information. What isn't in the deposition is that after the weird gum-kiss thing in the store, two months go by when things are back to what passes for normal in our house. Waldy celebrates Hanukah and Christmas with our family. She even comes on our skiing vacation to Aspen. So I sort of relax again and feel okay about having someone, her, there for us.

By then, besides working in the store, Waldy keeps Mom company during the day and takes her to various appointments. The level of tension in our family goes way down. As for me, I like it that Waldy hugs me, brushes my hair and tells me I'm pretty. I even like it when she calls me "baby" and lets me sit on her lap. I suppose I want to be someone's baby, as late as it is for me to get around to that. What I don't know then is that I am going to have to pay a high price for these two months of attention and affection.

Here's the public defender referring to what took place between me and Waldy after the gum-kiss.

Q: Okay. Well, this happened once. When was the next time something of an inappropriate physical or sexual manner happened?

A: Sometimes she laid with us [me and Chase] until we fell asleep.

Q: You said you were all in bed and Waldina touched you inappropriately?

A: It was just like under the cover, you know, touching.

Q: In what respect was it inappropriate?

A: She touched my genital areas.

Q: Now when you say she touched your genital area, did she place her hand—

A: Yes.

Q: —on your vagina?

A: Yes.

Q: Okay. Did she take any portion of her hand and rather than touch your vagina, actually insert her finger into your vagina?

A: Correct. Yes.

Q: Was this the first time that she had inserted her finger into your vagina?

A: Correct.

Q: And did anything subsequently occur as a result of that penetration?

A: Not that time.

Q: Okay, so you had no bleeding?

A: Correct.

Q: Now when she did this to you, your brother was there?

A: Yes. And it happened several times after that.

Q: Was he awake?

A: I'm sure most of the time he was.

Q. Did you say anything to her like stop; don't do it; what are you doing?

A: No, because I trusted her.

And I did trust her—then.

That night, like most, I'd helped Chase get ready for bed. Often, Waldy and I would both lie with him until he fell asleep. So I'm not surprised to see her walk in just as Chase is drifting off. She lies down behind me, and slowly reaches up my nightgown. *What's going on?* I think, panicking. Then she touches my breasts, and I get even more tense. I don't want to speak and wake up Chase, so I just lie there and hope she stops. But then she reaches into my underpants and sticks her finger in my vagina. Now I'm terrified. I want to scream, but I can't find my voice. It's like it's gone.

After minutes of this, while I am still lying there frozen, Waldy gets up and leaves. Maybe, because I haven't responded, she realizes that she made a mistake. I'm shaking in fear—at what just happened, but also because she's angry, and so maybe will now pack up and leave. So I get up and go after her, into her room.

"Why did you do that?" I ask.

"It's good for you. Now you'll know what to expect when you have a boyfriend," she explains in the calmest voice.

I can't imagine that what she's saying is true. But then, what do I know? I've never had a real boyfriend. Waldy is thirty; she must know more about this stuff than me. Maybe I should ask her to teach me about sex. I stand there for a long time, saying nothing.

"You didn't like it, so I stopped. Don't you want me to stop?"

In my panicked state, all I could think was, *Stop what?* I didn't want her to stop hugging and kissing me when I got home from school. I didn't want her to stop caring about me. What was in my mind was the question, *Who will love me if Waldy isn't here?* I was naive but, on some level, I knew that *if I don't give Waldy what she wants, she isn't going to give me what I need. And she'll probably take off.*

"Don't leave me," I say.

"I'm not going anywhere. Come lie down with me."

I go over to her bed and lie down. She pulls off my underpants and climbs on the bed between my legs. Then she uses her fingers to open the lips of my vagina and puts her tongue there. She does it for what feels like a long time, although I can't tell you for certain how long. This is a kid who hasn't gotten around to discovering her own genitals for the purpose of masturbation. So you can imagine how utterly bizarre I find my first experience of oral sex, or, if you prefer, "cunnilingus." Even when I gave my deposition, I didn't know that word.

If you're shocked, I don't blame you. When this was happening, I was in an altered state of fright and bewilderment, and filled with unfamiliar sensations. Some of them were even pleasurable, which only added to my simultaneous feelings of being out of control and under Waldy's. When the sex was occurring, even this first time, I knew what she was doing was wrong, and that I should not be letting her touch me like that. I remember having the strange thought, *This is probably what it would be like if I had sex with my mother.* But I was caught between two opposing fears. Fear one was that I was doing something perverted and dirty, for which I'd be heavily punished. Fear two was that if I stopped her, she'd leave me and I'd be really lonely again.

From the point when I was nearly seventeen and finally told someone about my abuse until not that long ago, I've questioned my actions and reactions that night countless times. It's what victims do, until we've healed enough to lay the blame squarely where it belongs: on our abusers. Looking back at that night, I see that even Waldy's question, "Do you want me to stop?" was pure manipulation on her part. In that moment, she knew exactly who she was dealing with and played with me like a puppeteer.

In the deposition, you can hear the public defender trying to shift the blame from Waldy to me. It happens all the time in child sexual abuse and rape cases. That's why we have to make sure the legal system does a better job of protecting victims, particularly minors, who gather the courage to report the crimes committed against them. We have to make sure that the justice system prosecutes the accused perpetrators, and *not the victims a second time.*

In the language of recovery, my job now as an adult survivor is to keep parenting "Little Lauren," so that she knows I understand why she did what she did back then, when she felt so sad. I understand that she was a double victim: of her mother's neglect and Waldy's abuse.

Another huge part of my ongoing recovery is unraveling this fear of being alone, which I still wrestle with today; the very same fear that made me vulnerable to Waldy's abuse thirteen years ago. During those years, I was terrified of Waldy leaving me without her protection from the chaos caused by my mother's emotional instability. The irony is that I was more isolated when I counted on Waldy to protect me than at any time before or since.

I did things that ended up being very damaging to me, because I was so desperately needy and deathly afraid of her leaving. Therapists call it a fear of abandonment. I was one of those people who, to my own detriment, walked around not knowing that this fear was the thing driving many of my choices. It's like when you stay in a bad relationship because you believe it's better than the alternative of being by yourself. Well, you can't be loved by anyone else unless you love yourself. Many of us grow up in families where we have to learn this the hard way. But the point of living just may be to get this lesson learned *however you can*. It's really what the rest of my story is about. How I came to love myself, so that now I can help others who face the same challenges I've had to overcome.

4

My Parallel Lives

Spring, 1998

I'm lying on the sofa with loose pillows covering me up to my chin, sniffling and wiping away tears.

"Pipsqueak,"—Dad stops on his way through the family room—"why are you crying?"

I put down my book. "I just feel so sad."

"About what?"

"Did you know that Anne Frank died just one month before the allies liberated her concentration camp?"

"Oh . . . you're reading her diary." He sits down on the end of the sofa, looks at me and then away at the dark TV screen across from us.

"Have you read it?"

"Yes, of course," he answers, then turns back to face me. "You know, her father survived Auschwitz. And got her diary published so we'd all know her story and what Hitler did to the Jews.

"Is Hitler why Grandpa came to America?"

"Your great grandfather came here from Eastern Europe before

Hitler," Dad says. "By doing that, he made it possible for Grandpa to be a dentist and me to be a lawyer. Next you and Sam and Chase will choose what you want to be." Dad's words are upbeat, but his face looks drawn and he isn't smiling.

"Never forget how fortunate you are, pipper. Otherwise, we dishonor Anne Frank and all the others who were lost."

"I know that."

"Is your homework all done?"

"This *is* my homework."

"Oh. Then I'll leave you to it," he says getting up. Looking around the room—"Did I leave a phone in here?"

"I heard something vibrate under the newspapers," I say, pointing to the pile on the coffee table.

He lifts the pile of papers and finds it.

"I'll be gone before you're up in the morning." Dad leans in and kisses my forehead. "Oh, I signed your report card; it's on the refrigerator. You make me proud, as usual." Then he reaches into his pocket. "Here's a bonus for your allowance," he says as he hands me a ten-dollar bill. "Don't spend it all in one place."

"Thanks, Daddy."

"I love you, pipper."

Since I'm average smart, I've had to work really hard in school for my straight As. My stellar academic performance continued throughout the years of my abuse, a testimony to the feat of compartmentalization I managed. It's one of those survival tactics people use when they have something really shitty going on in one compartment of their lives, say, living with an abuser at home, but not in another. At school, I can take a breather and sometimes shine. When I'm in class or hanging out at Power Smoothie with my friends, I can be a thirteen-year-old kid and not think about that other secret life.

Unfortunately, during this period Waldy starts exerting tighter control over me. She texts me several times during the day and shows up the minute school is out to drive me home. She even drops in to the school cafeteria at lunchtime to check up on me. At home, she drives deeper wedges between me and my sister and my mother, so I won't have anyone but her. Even though there were divisions before Waldy came, she sees that it's in her interest to make them wider.

How did she do it? Once, I told her not to pick me up, since I was going to the track meet after school to see Sam run the hundred meters. But then Waldy showed up at the regular time and talked me out of going to the meet, saying, "Sam never goes to your things. Why should you go to hers?" Many times, Waldy would purposely get Sam in trouble with Dad, telling him that she made us late for school in the morning, or that she teased Chase and made him cry. Dad would believe Waldy and make Sam go to her room as punishment. And even though *I knew* that Waldy was lying about Sam's misbehavior, I went along with these charades. Looking back, I feel bad about those times with Sam, but I also now understand that it was all part of Waldy's grooming of me. I got to be the special "good girl" who never did wrong, and so got more than my share of Dad's approval and Waldy's "treats." It's a wonder that Sam and I can be close sisters today; that our relationship survived so much pathological undermining.

Another time, Waldy told me something that Mom supposedly said; about how Mom hired the gardener to be a hit man and have Dad killed. My mother is a lot of things, but a murderer is not one of them. The sad part is I half believed Waldy (at first), and worried about it. Well, of course it wasn't true. Waldy took some rant of Mom's and twisted it into a lie. But I guess it served her purposes to make me worry about it.

No doubt you're wondering how all this abuse went on in our house under everyone's noses without anything being detected? Sadly, it wasn't that difficult for Waldy to pull off. After that first time on her bed, it became routine, maybe five out of seven nights a week. At first, she restrained herself when Dad was home, but eventually she started doing it any time of the day or night, whenever she could get me away from the rest of the family for as little as ten minutes. When I got older, I learned the word "quickie" to describe when couples have a short romp in bed or anywhere else, so one or both can get off the way Waldy got off with me.

That was my introduction to "making love": five or ten minutes of yucky sex in Waldy's quarters in exchange for another twenty-four hours of the care and affection I craved from her—or anyone. A strange, sick bargain for sure. Here's how she worked it.

We might be alone in the kitchen, Waldy loading the dishwasher while I put the clean load away. If she says, "Okay, let's go," that means I'm supposed to follow her into her bedroom or her bathroom, which is between her room and the pool. Once the door is locked, my pants come off, and I lie on the floor or on the rug, where she fingers me or uses her tongue on my vagina and clitoris. When she's touching me, she breathes hard; sometimes she sighs or moans, even though it's just her doing things to me.

But that's about to change. You see, when Waldy is raping me, I'm trying to keep my thoughts elsewhere, anywhere—it's a survival mechanism all abused kids use. The problem is that Waldy assumes I'm being a good little student, paying attention to what she's doing to me, so I'll know how to do the same things to her. On the day this becomes clear, we're in her bedroom; actually I am crouched, naked, on the rug with my arms tight around my knees, watching her while she takes off her clothes. *God, she's huge,* I think as I watch. It's the first time I've seen Waldy completely naked.

"Come on out here, baby," she says in a cooing voice.

I get up slowly and take the few steps to the bed where she's now lying, leaning back on her elbows. I shiver, the hair on my neck standing up, but not because of the air conditioning, which is on maximum, as it always is in our house. I'm scared of what's happening; how things are about to change between me and Waldy. She pulls my arm away from my chest and puts my hand between her legs. Her scratchy matted pubic hair and the wetness of her vagina are unfamiliar. My own hair is barely there, and soft. I want to pull my hand away from her crotch, but she keeps guiding my fingers with hers, moving them rhythmically up and down.

"Just like how I do it to you." Then she leans back. "Go ahead, rub my pussy."

Up until that moment, I had naively thought it was my choice whether or not I would reciprocate and do these things to Waldy. I pull my hand away saying, "I don't want to."

She sits straight up, scowling at me. "That's not very nice of you, is it?"

Then she's on her feet and grabbing my forearm. "Not after all I've done to make you feel good, you little bitch."

"Ow, that hurts," I cry out as she twists my arm and pushes me facedown on her bed. "Stop it, please." I'm petrified as my face lands flat on the edge of her bed, halfway off, so I'm looking at the stitching in the navy blue carpet and the pink palm trees filling the wallpaper on the adjoining wall.

"Where'd you get the idea this was going to be a one-way street?" I hear her saying, as she walks to another part of the room and then comes back. Then she grabs my body and shoves me, so I'm wedged into the space between her bed frame and the wall. There's silence before I feel a whack on my buttocks, then two or three more on my lower back. Sharp pricks alternate with a smooth, hard surface hitting my skin. She's hitting me with her hairbrush.

I cry out loudly, one time.

"Shut your fucking mouth," she says, climbing onto the bed next to me to put her hand over my mouth. "You think someone's going to come to my door? If they do, I'll just tell them it's my TV."

When she takes her hand from my mouth, I don't dare make a peep. With my head still facedown in the crack, I hear her walk another few steps. The wait is excruciating, imagining how she might hurt me next. The answer is beyond anything I can imagine. With a grunt, she pushes on the opposite side of the bed, so I'm crushed between the frame and the wall. There's a piercing pain in my skull, and I'm dazed and terrified, but I dutifully remain mute. All the while, I'm studying the pattern on the wallpaper, wishing I could make myself disappear. I hear pieces of her sentences . . . "make me do this" . . . "love you" . . . "your own good." Finally I hear no sounds other than the roar of trains entering a station—the throbbing in my head and neck reverberating up and down both sides of my body.

Another minute or two goes by before she pulls on my arm and lifts me up and out of the crack. Propped up next to her on the bed, I feel like somebody's rag doll. When I lift my head and dare to look, I see her eyes moving up and down my side and back. Later, I realize that when Waldy beat me, she took care to keep any potential bruises out of sight, safely limited to my torso or buttocks where, given my age, no one ever looked.

Finally, she pushes the hair out of my face, saying in a syrupy tone, "You shouldn't have made me do that. You know how much I love you. But I had to teach you a lesson. I did it for your own good. Do you understand why I had to do that?"

I'm still frozen in terrified silence, until I realize from her expectant look that I'm supposed to answer. "Yes."

"What do you say?"

"I'm sorry."

"Will you do what I tell you now?"

"Yes."

So I do, and afterward she takes me in her arms and spoons with me in her bed, rocking me and saying soothing things in my ear.

The morning after that awful night, I pop out of bed when Waldy wakes us and I act like nothing happened. I shower and allow her to do my hair—yes, with the same brush. Then I have a sleepy breakfast with my brother and sister. I continue to act normal as the three of us get in the car with Waldy for the twenty-minute drive to school during which Chase, as usual, entertains us with his favorite knock-knock jokes and car games.

I won't try to explain Waldy's behavior. I'll let it speak for itself.

But why, you may be wondering, didn't I run the hundred feet down the hall to where my mother was sleeping alone (Dad being away) to tell her there was a deranged nanny in our house who just beat me up? Why didn't I immediately call Dad? I wanted to tell my parents, but I was too ashamed and confused. Since I hadn't told them as soon as it all started, I was afraid they would they think I had wanted Waldy to touch me. I wondered, would they think I was gay? What if Dad got so mad, he attacked Waldy and went to jail? I couldn't risk it; we loved and needed him so much. So I just kept quiet, thinking it was what I had to do.

The fact is when I finally left Waldy's room that night, I went straight into the family room and wrote a thousand-word essay for English class. Then I fell into bed next to Chase and went right to sleep. By the next morning (I remember it as my first "morning after"), I'm 100 percent Waldy's prisoner. I don't see a way out of the situation.

When I get to school the next day, I'm relieved to be in seventh-grade English class, where we're talking about Anne Frank's diary. We've each been assigned to pick one paragraph that reveals something important about Anne's character. When my teacher Ms. Martin asks who wants to read, I raise my hand. My choice of a paragraph is from a part of the diary where Anne sounds more like a lonely girl than a stoic heroine. When what hurts her is more personal than the war or the genocide taking place right below her family's attic hiding place.

"Please stand up when you read," Ms. Martin says.

As I get to my feet, I'm feeling a little shaky, but my calm returns as soon as I start reading.

> *Crying can bring some relief, as long as you don't cry alone. Despite all my theories and efforts, I miss—every day and every hour of the day—having a mother who understands me. That's why with everything I do and write, I imagine the kind of mom who doesn't take everything people say too seriously,*

but who does take me seriously. I find it difficult
to describe what I mean but the word "mom" says
it all.

There's another sentence to the paragraph, but I sit down because my eyes are filling up with tears, making it hard to see the words on the page.

"What does that passage tell you about Anne, Lauren?"

"It tells me that Anne feels invisible to her mom."

"Thank you, Lauren. Who wants to read next?"

At the end of class, Ms. Martin collects our essays, and then, as I'm packing up to leave, she asks me to come up to her desk.

"Is everything all right at home, Lauren?"

"Yeah, things are okay," I say. I drop my eyes down to look at my sneakers and notice one lace is untied. When I meet her gaze, she's twisting her mouth and tilting her head to one side as if she's waiting for me to say more. I use my blank look to try and deflect what I expect to be her next probing question.

"Is your mother still living at home?"

"Uh-huh."

"And the woman who picks you up in the afternoon is your—?"

"Nanny . . .Waldy."

"How's that working out?"

No one who deals with my mother thinks things are fine at our house. The school principal and teachers who've had Sam, Chase or me in their classes have heard her fly off the handle when they call home to schedule a parent meeting or inquire why we're absent. Some of them also know about the six months that Mom was gone after Chase was born, just like they eventually find out whenever my parents' marriage goes from bad to worse and Mom moves out of the house and into an apartment. But then she always comes back, and things go on as before.

Sometimes, like that day, I wish there was someone I *could* talk to about what's going on in my life. But I can't, because the rule in our family is to keep private things private. And then, as you know, I have my own reasons for not telling Ms. Martin about Waldy.

"The nanny is working out fine," I answer with a forced smile.

"Okay. I look forward to reading your essay on Anne Frank."

"Thanks," I say. As I walk down the hall to my next class, I'm pissed. *How can she be that gullible? It's so obvious I need help.*

Waldy has her own ideas about how to improve things at home. She's determined to indoctrinate me into thinking that she and I are no longer just nanny and child to each other. No, we've turned a corner and become a romantic couple, a future husband and wife. I've since learned that pedophiles, which is what Waldy is, are emotionally arrested at the age of the children they find sexually compelling.

When I came upon this psychological insight in one of the many books I've read about sexual predators since all this unfolded, it rang true. It's the only way I can understand what might have been going on inside Waldy's sick mind back then. She was a grown woman with the emotional capacity of a twelve- or thirteen-year-old, but with the aggression and entitlement of an adult woman who identified as a man. She may or may not be a lesbian. It really doesn't matter.

I do believe that something monstrous, probably sexual and violent happened to Waldy at a young age. But I don't know that for sure, and it's not my job to find "the reason" to explain her behavior. At the same time, when I'm consumed with anger and loathing about what she did to me, the likelihood that she too was abused when she was young helps me. The rage comes back when, in the course of my work today with the Lauren's Kids Foundation, I hear about other children being sexually preyed on. I need to let go of that anger for my own good. Although those negative feelings have their place when you're healing from abuse, they do me no good at this stage in my recovery.

At the time I'm writing about, when the sexual and physical abuse has only just begun, this notion of Waldy's that we are "lovers" is one I buy hook, line and sinker. I suppose it allows me to cope with the sexual acts she demands of me by combining them with my own budding romantic fantasies. Whatever the reasons, when Waldy calls me her *bonita gringa*, I become someone else, a person who literally belongs to Waldy. I am no longer my parents' daughter, Lauren. No longer do I think of myself as a young woman with her own romantic and sexual life ahead of her to explore at the appropriate time with a boy or man her own age. I'm Waldy's girlfriend and future wife. Waldy's indoctrination of me is accomplished in a matter of a few months. Later, no one had to explain to me why Patty Hearst joined her captors after spending forty-five days in a closet, and robbed that bank. I totally understood. The medical term I've learned since is "Stockholm syndrome," referring to a kidnap victim's state of mind after a long period of imprisonment, when he or she begins to identify with his or her captor.

It's a Saturday morning, and the rest of the family is out of the house—Dad and Chase with Sam at her soccer game, Mom at Confection Connection. I'm sitting with Waldy on her bed. On the

TV, a buff man and a woman with enormous boobs are "doing it." While corny music plays, the man, who has an enormously long penis (although I've never seen any other adult's penis at this point in my life), moves it in and out of her for an incredibly long time. While at first I find this fascinating, as it drags on and nothing more happens, I'm bored.

At least, in the beginning, there's a little skit about the man coming to the door dressed in a UPS uniform. He delivers a box containing a flimsy black negligee. The woman opens the box and puts on her new negligee so he can ogle her. After she gets excited, she tears off his uniform and he gets rid of her negligee. They kiss for a minute before he pushes her down on the dining room table, where they start screwing. I guess that eventually gets uncomfortable, because then she hops off the table and takes him by the hand into her bedroom, where they're still going at it.

"What do you think of that?" Waldy's fingers climb up my arm as she awaits my answer.

"What do you mean?"

"We could do it the same way."

"But he has a penis. So . . .?"

"Silly, we don't need a real one."

"Oh." I don't know what she means, but I dread what's coming next.

After she shuts off the porn video, Waldy turns our sex into an hours-long ordeal, introducing objects, beginning with a fake rubber penis (I'd never heard of or seen a dildo before). If she thinks that watching the video has warmed me up, she's miscalculated. By the time she slathers some creamy stuff on the fake penis and tries to stick it in my vagina, my body is rebelling. Even after I mentally tell my vagina to relax, I can't make it open up. On one level, I'm amazed that a body part has a mind of its own. If only the rest of me could fight back, too. But very soon it becomes clear that any resisting, intentional or not, will only make things worse, because Waldy then assumes I'm doing it on purpose and becomes even more determined to get what she wants.

"Stay right there. Don't move," she says in a voice I take to mean "don't even think about getting away."

When she comes back with a long carrot and a cucumber in her hands, I have a realization that startles me. *She's done this before. She's done these same things to other children before me.* I don't know why this occurs to me right then. Perhaps it's just seeing her come up with all these tricks so effortlessly. It doesn't take long after that for her to accomplish her goal for that day. And as she's shoving things inside me and asking me if it feels good, I soon learn to say "yes, yes, yes." It's the only way to get to the end of the ordeal.

I apologize if you find this upsetting. I don't blame you. It's no fun to dredge these incidents back up and remember the way I felt when they were happening. I'm only sharing enough for you to understand the insidious nature of this abuse, and how it puts a kid's body and mind into a state of passivity and fear, not unlike the victim of a kidnapping who develops Stockholm syndrome.

Everything I'm describing to you that Waldy did to me is true, but, tragically, none of it is so unusual. The same crimes are happening to girls and boys all over this country and around the world. Just turn on the TV. It happens everywhere: Jaycee Dugar, kidnapped at eleven and held a sexual prisoner for eighteen years in California; Sean Hornbeck, taken and kept for four years in Missouri; and the young woman in Austria, whose father kept her in their basement so he could rape her whenever he pleased. At least they all survived. As you know, many others don't. I was horrified when I learned that the most common age for girls to be sexually abused is under three. I get calls in my foundation office all the time from mothers or day-care teachers who discover a baby girl's genital bruises and have to report a father, stepfather or another relative for the crime of incest. Then we have to find help for the child, and there's always a waiting list at our county shelters and counseling centers.

If you're still reading, I guess you're curious about how I managed to go from the weak, pathetic state I was in at this point to strong enough to stand up for myself and report my abuser. I'll get there, I promise. But because it's so hard for people to understand why kids don't tell right away when they're being abused, I also need to account for those years in between and show you what took me so long. As was true for me, I've learned that the number one fear that keeps kids from telling is their fear of losing the only parent or caretaker they have. They're also afraid of not being believed.

But there's more to it than these fears. I've talked to doctors and scientists who have studied abused children, and they point to other mind-body factors that keep kids from reporting people who are regularly hurting them. They tell me that when children are physically or sexually abused, their brains literally change—and not for the better.

Here's what happens: a part of the brain called the hippocampus, which turns sensory experiences into memories, gets flooded with the hormones that the body naturally releases to help you escape danger, the "fight or flight" chemicals everyone has. When this flooding happens repeatedly, the brain's memory center shrinks and works less well. This explains why memories of childhood sexual abuse are often forgotten, or repressed, until they're triggered later in adulthood. And given the age when most girls and boys are abused, you can see how many abusers get away with their crimes, and why it sometimes takes a long time for victims to remember their own experiences and ask for help.

I'm certainly not claiming I was lucky to have been abused. But since those are the cards I was dealt, I've figured out how to use the bad for good in my life. I see that a lot of the strength I have today comes from the fighting I had to do to get free of my abuser, and then get justice. It takes enormous effort to enter and stay in the process of recovery from child abuse or incest. Because I've had to do that work, I've received the gift of emotional self-awareness that comes with it. I ask you to keep these positive things in mind as we continue through the darker parts of my journey.

5

Telling Right from Wrong

May, 1998

"Did you hear about the seventh-grade teacher who got arrested for having sex with her student?" Stacey and I are in gym class on the soccer field, waiting our turn to practice dribbling and passing. The sun is high overhead, the temperature already in the upper eighties.

"Yeah," I say, trying to sound casual, as if this is not a topic I've thought a lot about.

"Do you believe it?" she asks.

"Sure. I saw the teacher on the cover of *People* and her boyfriend was just on *Oprah*."

"Well I don't get it."

"What about it don't you get?" I ask as I wonder how I might feel about Mary Kay Letourneau and her twelve-year-old lover if my life was different.

"It would be like Ms. Martin doing it with Scott or Brandon. Doesn't that seem weird to you?"

"If I heard it was Ms. Martin, yes, it would be very weird."

I'm aware of walking a tightrope, careful not to say anything that might make Stacey suspicious. But I don't like lying to her. She's my only friend.

Coach Cooper blows his whistle. "Lauren, Stacey, let's go."

We dash out onto the field, me in front. Coach kicks us the ball. I dribble it a few yards and pass to Stacey, who uses her thigh to send it right back at me. She and I trade some more passes before I give the ball a final hard kick, sending it right into the hands of the goalie, who tosses it back into play with a smirk on her face.

"How about using some strategy, girls?" Coach Cooper yells from midfield. "You won't score any points that way."

Stacey giggles. I smile sheepishly. My mind is not on soccer. Neither is Stacey's, apparently. She picks up right where she left off as we begin our long walk back to the other end of the field.

"What I really don't get is why they arrested the teacher for rape. I mean . . . how could she rape him, anyway?"

"Duh? It's easy. They've got all the right body parts to do it."

"But I thought rape means someone forcing you to have sex with them." She uses her gym shirt to wipe the sweat off her brow and then stops walking and turns toward me, waiting for my answer.

"Not always," I begin nervously. "I think they arrested Mary Kay because she's in her thirties and he's in the sixth grade. So they figure she tricked him into it. But I heard him say on *Oprah* that it was all okay with him because he loves her."

"He loves her!" Stacey repeats incredulously. "I doubt that. My little brother is in sixth grade and, well, I don't think I've ever heard him or any of his friends say they love anybody except maybe the Dolphins if they're winning or the centerfold from a *Playboy* they've sneaked into the house."

"Beats me," I say and resume walking, hoping Stacey is done talking about this.

No such luck.

"Okay, what would you do if Coach Cooper wanted to do it with you?"

"Are you nuts?" I blurt out looking to the center of the field where Coach is shouting at another pair of runners. Admittedly, he is kind of good-looking in a crew cut, Marine sort of way.

Stacey adds, "He's really cute, I mean, for his age."

"So what?" I respond with a shrug.

"So . . . what if the deal was he would give you an easy A and then you wouldn't have to get all sweaty in class because you'd be his secret girlfriend?"

In spite of my discomfort, I let myself think through Stacey's hypothetical proposition, until I get to the part where I'd have to actually let Coach Cooper touch me. I cringe. "No way," I say. "It wouldn't be worth it. Anyway, why are you asking me this stuff?"

"Because you're my best friend. Somebody else might think I'm a pervert if I was to talk about this stuff with them."

This wasn't the first conversation I'd had about Mary Kay Letourneau. Her arrest in Washington State for raping her twelve-year-old student had been all over the news for months, especially when she got caught doing it with him a second time after promising not to, and then had his baby. Most people don't buy the story that Mary Kay and her boyfriend, Vili, love each other. Even Oprah gives Vili the raised-eyebrow treatment, asking him if he's sure he's old enough to know what love means when he swears to it on her show. A judge gave Mary Kay seven years in prison for what she did. But on *Oprah*, Vili says he's going to wait for her. At the time, I thought that was very loyal of him.

Waldy holds my hand tightly during that entire episode of *Oprah*. We're sitting on her bed, both of us glued to the screen. When pictures of Mary Kay in her orange prison suit are shown on screen, Waldy gasps. "That's what they'll do to me if you tell anyone." Then she releases my hand.

I let it drop onto the bed and turn to check out her expression. Her lips are tight, in a firm, straight line, and she's squinting, like she's trying to look right through me. I'm scared. I wonder, *What does she want to hear from me?*

"I haven't told anyone," I say, hoping to be believed.

"Not yet," Waldy says with a deeply furrowed brow.

It's true. I haven't said a word to anyone. But there is one close call when Waldy and I are almost caught in the act. We're in her room. There's sex going on between us when we're interrupted by a knock on the door, then Sam's voice: "Waldy, Mom wants you."

Waldy pushes me off the bed and shoos me into her closet, where I stand off to the side with the sliding door partly open, watching while Waldy hastily puts on her clothes and goes to the door. Instead of waiting out in the hall as Waldy probably expected, Sam walks into the room to finish delivering her message.

"She wants you to make dinner early cuz she's going to the store," she says brusquely. As Sam turns to leave, I swear she sees me out of the corner of her eye. But she doesn't say a word.

I dress as fast as I can, and hurry down the hall to the kitchen.

As soon as I sit down next to Chase at the table, Mom, tilting her head to the side, lips pursed, asks, "What were you doing in Waldy's closet?"

"She was just helping me pick out some clothes," I answer,

lying automatically. Mom gives me another once-over, but despite the illogic of my statement, says nothing more about the incident.

"Pour Chase a glass of milk, please," she says.

When I get up and walk past Sam on my way to the refrigerator, she lifts her eyebrows and gives me a quizzical look. In retrospect, I realize that Sam was the only member of my family who caught on to my abuse long before I told. But no one paid attention to her when she questioned Waldy's behavior in incidents like this one. It's sad and too typical of what happens in families when abuse is happening. All these years later, I want to thank her for trying to help me. It took courage.

My discussion with Waldy about Mary Kay Letourneau during the *Oprah* show is the first time she and I talk about the possibility of "our relationship" being found out, and what might happen if it ever is.

"You don't want them to send me to jail, do you?" she asks.

"No," I answer in the tone of a much younger child who knows she's done something wrong, even if she doesn't get what it is.

"That's good, but there's something else you need to understand." She takes my chin in the palm of her hand to make direct eye contact. "It won't only be me who's sent away if they find out."

"What do you mean?" I truly don't know what she's saying.

"You'll be sent away, too, before a week goes by. Your father is not going to want any news about his lezzy daughter hitting the newspapers."

"But I'm not a lesbian," I say without thinking.

She laughs, but not like she thinks it's funny. She gives me a sideways look. "I have news for you, my little *gringa*. You are what you do, not what you say."

I don't like Waldy calling me that. I don't see how I can be a lesbian, since the sex isn't my idea. But, as I said, by this time I belong to her. If she wants me to be her girlfriend, that's what I am. I know it's difficult for people who haven't experienced abuse to understand. When someone you love repeatedly and intentionally hurts you over a long period of time, you lose your identity. You are nothing, feel nothing and want nothing other than what the abuser tells you to be, feel and want.

Even though Mary Kay Letourneau chose a boy my age for her lover, their relationship is the closest thing I have then as a model for my secret life. Except in Waldy's and my version of the forbidden-love fairy tale, I'm the "wife" and the one who will have the babies, while Waldy plays my "husband" and our future babies' father.

Years later, I would read a book about the Letourneau case called *If Loving You Is Wrong*. Speaking from prison, Mary Kay says she and her student Vili share a "special relationship that no one else could possibly understand." The words could be right out of Waldy's mouth when she's trying to shape my view of our relationship. She makes it sound like what we have is beyond the ordinary, meaning rare and good, which also justifies why we have to keep it hidden, since "*they* just wouldn't understand."

Something that drives me crazy when I read it in that book concerns the way some people, egged on by the tabloid media, turn into groupies for Mary Kay, comparing the story of her and Vili's doomed relationship to *Romeo and Juliet*. And then others (mostly men but some women, too) call Vili "lucky" because he's been initiated into the "art of love" by a pretty older woman.

Well, no one calls *me* lucky when my abuse hits the newspapers in 2001. However, because mine involves a female abuser, many people try to minimize Waldy's crimes, just as they did in the Letourneau case. In nasty letters that come to our house or to my father's office, I'm called a "spoiled brat" for making a fuss over "so little." And I'm branded a "lesbian," as if this should somehow heighten my shame and persuade me to keep my mouth shut. It's a painful bind: on one hand, people seem to be saying it's my fault for "letting it happen," but then also insisting that since it's a woman perpetrator, no crime has actually been committed. And let's get another thing straight. The vast majority of boys who are molested by men don't turn into homosexuals because of it, and neither do girls when they're sexually abused by women (or men). Such violations can mess with our feelings about sex, but usually not in that way.

I hope my story helps dispel the myth that being the underage victim of a female sex offender is less traumatic than being raped by a man. If that's what you believe, you are missing the essential point about incest and child sexual abuse: that as bad as the physical acts of abuse are, the worst horror and the thing that causes the longest-lasting trauma for child victims is the violation of trust by a parent or some other caretaker who is close to him or her, like Waldy was to me.

Female sex offenders, most often mothers, go woefully under-reported. One result is that the abuse they commit stays under the radar, and lasts much longer for their victims. That means those victims face a burden even heavier than that of children who are sexually violated by their fathers. It's the persistent belief that mothers, except for a very few deranged females, never harm their children, because women are just not capable of crimes like the ones I'm describing. Think about it . . . your mom makes you her secret whore, available to be used for sexual gratification any time of the day or night. You were born of her body and you remain her private property. This is the woman you're supposed to go to for comfort. Your needs and feelings don't matter. It's the worst betrayal of all, and that's why people don't want to believe it, even about people they don't know.

I've heard from survivors of female sexual abuse who tried to report their abuse to counselors or ministers, but were not believed. Some were called perverts for thinking up such wicked stories. One desperate girl had to change the sex of who she said was sexually abusing her and say it was her father, before anyone would help her get out of her abusive situation. For victims of sexual abuse by mothers or mother figures—older sisters, aunts, grandmothers, babysitters, nuns or teachers—the feeling of loss and betrayal can be monumental. It keeps us in situations in which we're abused for many years. It makes reporting the crime to law enforcement authorities, the idea of putting "Mom" in jail, simply impossible to imagine. This is the awful dilemma I would eventually face with Waldy.

During my middle and early high school years, I buy into Waldy's fantastical version of our future life together, which crystallizes one afternoon while we're sitting in the car in the lower-school parking lot, waiting to pick up Chase from his Boy Scout troop meeting. As I look to either side of us at the other boys' mothers sitting in their SUVs and station wagons, waiting for their sons to emerge from the scout meeting, I feel an urge bubble up inside me to be just like them. It's a desire I'd always held close to my heart; that is, to be a mom. Not like my mother, but a "real" mom who adores her kids and always puts their needs first. It remains to this day the most important wish I have for my life, but I don't think I'd ever spoken the words aloud to anyone before that day in the parking lot with Waldy.

"I want to have my own kids," I say. "I want to be a real mother."

"You will," Waldy assures me.

"But . . . they'll be laughed at if they have two women for parents. I don't want my kids to go through that."

"They won't. Things are changing. By the time you get out of high school and get your money, it'll be legal for two women or two men to marry." She pats my hand and smiles.

"Really?"

"I wouldn't lie to you about something so important."

There is at least one outrageous thing in what Waldy says that day. It's not the idea that same-sex marriage will someday be legal. It's already legal in several states and, as far as I'm concerned, that's fine. The outrageous part is Waldy's expectation that when I turn eighteen, the two of us will somehow walk away from my family hand in hand with a large sum of money. I never said a word to Waldy about an inheritance, because in our family we didn't talk about money. Besides, I had no information that I would inherit any amount of money when I turned eighteen. This "when you get your money" notion is entirely Waldy's. I never question her about it because I fear what she will do to me if I do. Clearly, in her fantasy world, Waldy thinks of me and my father's money as her lifelong meal tickets.

So during the time I'm living this strange, parallel reality, I try on the role of Waldy's wife and the future mother of our children, as if it's a costume I might wear next Halloween. I think most pre-pubescent girls enjoy such "when I grow up to be a woman" fantasies. They envision their wedding to the man of their dreams and see themselves pushing a stroller with other young mothers.

As an adult survivor, I've had to go back and reclaim that desire, which, now that I'm twenty-six, I cherish more than ever. I also cling to the idea, which may or may not be true, that I can heal the pain I felt back then as a lonely child by having my own children and adoring them as I always wanted to be adored. It's been hard enough to get past my embarrassment about the fantasies I had about my "relationship" with Waldy so that I can put these words down on the page. But disclosing all the feelings that went with the abuse is another important step in my process of self-disclosure and self-forgiveness. I now know that there was nothing wrong with my girlhood fantasies; the problem was the person manipulating them.

Another way I've chosen to work out this whole complicated jumble of feelings about wanting to be a mom is by creating the Lauren's Kids Foundation. I still hope to have my own children someday, but in the meantime I have 39 million kids I'm helping take care of. Sadly, that is the number of children who are survivors of sexual abuse in this country today. Having been one of them, when I hear this number now, I shiver.

For my fifteenth birthday, on October 12, Waldy makes me a two-layer chocolate-on-chocolate cake with the outline of a white swan on top. She, Mom and Dad, Chase and Sam sing "Happy

Birthday" while I blow out all sixteen candles, one for good measure, surrounding the swan.

"Don't forget to make a wish," Chase yells while I'm still blowing.

I haven't forgotten, but my wish probably ranks up there on the weirdness chart for a fifteen-year-old's birthday wishes: "Please, Waldy, stop making me have sex with you. And stop hurting me, but please don't stop loving me." I can't tell you to whom I'm sending this wish. Maybe it's going out to the good witch from *The Wizard of Oz.* I've just seen the movie on TV and identify with Dorothy being lost and in need of supernatural help. I've already pretty much given up on God, who doesn't seem to think my countless prayers, which are the same as my birthday wish but addressed to him, are worth granting.

A few weeks later, my mother hits one of her low points.

It's the Sunday before Halloween, and we're all in the kitchen carving pumpkins—Chase, Sam and I with Mom and Dad. It's an annual ritual in our family: we go to the pumpkin patch and pick out seven or eight good-sized pumpkins, then carve them up with different scary faces and put the finished pumpkins out in front of the house for the neighborhood trick-or-treaters.

This year, carving is well under way when Sam announces she's finished her pumpkin and has to go call her girlfriend Tricia, who just texted to say she has something important to tell her. Mom says she can call Tricia later; Sam protests, and it degenerates quickly from there. Mom gets sarcastic: "Oh, you poor little brat . . . now you can't talk to your little trashy girlfriend." Sam defends Tricia. Dad jumps in, telling Mom to "cut out the trash talk, Pat." Of course, Mom is furious that Dad has taken Sam's side, and throws her half-carved pumpkin across the table at him. Dad dodges it, and asks in a controlled voice, "Have you gone off your meds again?" This makes Mom go ballistic. She picks up her carving knife, but by then Dad's got her arm, and she drops it on the floor.

They go outside on the patio to finish their fight "in private." They needn't have bothered. Their yelling is loud enough for us to hear Mom say she's leaving him "for good." We know she doesn't really mean she's going for good, although by this point I think we all sort of wish she would. We just hate the constant arguing. When I look out the sliding-glass door, I see Mom flailing her arms, trying to hit Dad. Then he's on his phone, and the next thing I see are the flashing lights of a police car in front of the house

Waldy shows up in the kitchen just as Sam is leaving to go to her room, obviously relieved to have pumpkin carving over with. Waldy looks at the mess and shakes her head, giving us a "what happened now?" look.

"Mom threw her pumpkin at Dad," Chase explains. "Now they're outside fighting."

"Do you want me to help?" I ask, feeling bad that Waldy's stuck with the cleanup job.

"Just finish carving your pumpkin," she says, grabbing a dustpan and a mop from the closet and then squatting to scoop up the pieces on the floor. "It's bath time for Chase."

Meanwhile, outside a discussion is had with the officers, and everyone calms down. By the time Mom and Dad come back in to finish their pumpkins, the kitchen is cleaned up.

Just as our family passes for normal to anyone who doesn't know better, I probably seem like a pretty average ninth grader, with one exception. I never have friends over to our house, and I rarely go out to socialize with anyone, not after school or on weekends. Instead, I stay home and do my homework and spend my free time with Waldy and Chase. Our family, by this point, is pretty fragmented. Although Mom has handed over the operation of Confection Connection to her employees, when she's living at home, she's rarely awake and around the house the same times we are. Sam has turned into a total jock who plays soccer in the fall and track in the spring, and is a star in both sports. The rest of the time, she's with her friends. That's fine with Waldy, who's suspicious of Sam's possible suspicions, and doesn't encourage her to spend any time with us. Chase, who's only nine, poses no threat to Waldy.

In fact, the three of us—Waldy, Chase and I—have formed a little family unit within our household. After school, we watch TV, go swimming or play videogames. When we leave the house, it's to play soccer at the park or go bowling, and then eat out after at the burger joint. We usually get some takeout for Sam to eat when she comes home from practice. And all this time, behind this facade of a normal, busy and happy-enough household, I'm still Waldy's secret sex slave.

Where's my father in all this, you wonder? Dad works until eight or nine most nights, with the exception of Sundays, when he turns off his phones and we become a *Brady Bunch* episode for the day. I joke, but I believe this weekly connection with my dad is probably what keeps me sane during this otherwise crazy time. There are many times when, if one of us has a school play or a recital while Dad has to be up in Tallahassee, he will charter a plane for the evening, just so he won't miss an important event. From Dad's perspective, and ours, too, he's just a workaholic father doing his best to provide for us.

Still, I can look back and wish that he had been there more

often, and had saved me from Waldy—*and* from my mother's mood swings. Maybe he should have separated from Mom permanently, or made her go into formal treatment as a condition of staying at home with us. But that wasn't really what married people did then, at least not as far as he knew. He was providing for his family, and he couldn't be everywhere at once. I know that to this day, the fact that he missed what Waldy was doing to me in those years continues to torture him. And that makes me sad.

In the midst of the darkness and confusion that feels endless during my eighth- and ninth-grade years, I have one moment of clarity and inspiration when I find a cause I can believe in. It happens on a Friday night, while all of us kids are with Dad watching TV. On the show *20/20*, correspondent Robin Roberts does a report on displaced Rwandan child refugees who are stuck in an orphanage, six years after the war that killed most of their parents. Some of the surviving teenagers have missing limbs because of the genocide they lived through. Now they have nothing and look so alone, and yet somehow they're brave and hopeful. The show breaks for a commercial advertising laundry detergent, leaving me very upset.

"That's so awful! How can we sit here and do nothing when those kids have to live like that?"

"There's nothing we can do," Sam answers, grabbing the remote. "I'm switching to *America's Funniest Home Videos*. You had your turn."

"But it's not over—"

Dad, who's been listening and half-watching while reading the newspaper in his recliner, interrupts. "Sam, let her finish the show." Then to me: "What would you do if you could do something for them?"

The idea comes to me instantly. "I'd raise money to get them more food and clothes and maybe even some toys."

"Okay, then do it," he says.

At school the next day, I go straight to the principal to request permission to launch a new club: Rwandans We Do Care. Once it's official, I have copies of the *20/20* show made and send them to all the schools in Broward County. At my school, I give talks to social studies classes to pick up some more volunteers. Then there are about a dozen of us who make flyers and set up a table in front of school, to raise money from parents as they pick up and drop off their kids. By Christmas, we've raised nearly $10,000 from our school and others. Monsignor Walsh from Miami's Catholic archdiocese comes to our school to formally accept the funds we raised, which are to be distributed to African orphanages where Rwandan children like the ones I saw on *20/20* are living. After that, I learn about the problem of landmines maiming kids who live in former war zones like Bosnia and Afghanistan, and I raise some more money for an organization trying to get rid of them.

At the end of the school year, when I tell Dad the total amount I've raised, he's very impressed. "Really, that much? You're quite the organizer, pipper. You'll see that it's a valuable skill once you get out in the real world."

I'm actually the one who's the most surprised by my success with these projects, the first causes I've ever taken on. It helps me discover my ability to stick to something, and not waver off course when the going gets tough. But I see this quality as a double-edged sword. I'm stubborn, and I sometimes stick to the wrong people and things that hurt me, like my secret pact with Waldy. But the same perseverance helps me do good things, too. It took a while, but eventually I learned how to tell the difference between good and bad stubbornness, and came to understand that I have the right to extricate myself from something that doesn't feel right before I get drawn too far in. It's about trusting your gut, which probably isn't easy for anyone to learn, but it's especially hard for abused kids and adult survivors. The reasons are complicated.

Number one, our bodies do not belong to us for as long as the abuse goes on, and sometimes long after it has stopped. It's hard to trust your gut when you can't find it or feel it. Gut is another word for "solar plexus." This is a very sensitive part of the body that's important when you're doing yoga or meditation, or when you're under stress. It's where you focus your attention in order to center and ground yourself. That means feeling your two feet solidly on the ground and not being all zoned out, like you have to be when you're being abused. When you're being raped or beaten up, you have to cut off all feeling, lest you cry out in pain and risk another beating or other punishment. As a survivor, you have to work really hard to open up your solar plexus again and let the energy flow in and out. You have to learn all over again how to trust your gut naturally, the way that children do unless someone abuses them.

After working through a lot of my abuse, I can say that my body and instincts belong to me again, far more than they used to. Still, when I'm trying to make a decision for the foundation about whether to take a certain donation from a new person or company, I sometimes tell them that I need time to consider it before I give my answer. Not so much to think it through, but to feel my way through it. To do that, I go someplace where I can be alone and simply breathe. If I can exhale several deep breaths without feeling tightness in my chest or a pain in my stomach, I know that the person is probably okay. At least I know that there are no obvious bad vibes telling me I should stay away from this donor or volunteer.

I might not always be right in my conclusions, but at least I know they're mine.

August, 1999

If you're a kid, the first day of a new school year is the only New Year's Day that matters. Because this is my first day of high school, it's more like the beginning of the new millennium; never mind that the calendar won't officially turn to the year 2000 for another four months. On that blisteringly hot and muggy August Monday morning, I feel like I've been transformed into someone else as soon as I enter the upper-school gates, leaving middle school behind forever. Okay, I'm just fifteen and I don't drive yet, so I still have to be dropped off and picked up by Waldy. But my life feels different to me, like there's something or someone circling around me who represents change. But it's only on the periphery of my awareness.

As the days go by, I'm like a caged bird with a case of wanderlust who's just realized that the little metal door on my cage opens, even if only from the outside. Maybe I knew about the door before, but it didn't matter, since I haven't wanted to get out and explore as much as I'm beginning to now. It will still take someone other than me (and certainly not Waldy, my keeper) to open it.

There is someone: a boy named Kris Lim. But at this point, he (like me) can't imagine that within two years he'll become the one who liberates me from my cage. How could he know? The total sum of our contact so far has been sitting next to each other in earth science class. Our teacher Mr. Stewart is one of those science types who loves his subject so much, he has no idea how boring he sounds talking about it. So to pass the time, Kris asks to borrow a pencil and then draws pictures of Mr. Stewart under a pile of falling rocks. I give him a stick of my bubble gum and show him the games on my new flip-top cell phone. He texts me a joke. I text back an LOL. I ask him for the definition of "alluvium" (silt, pebbles, unconsolidated material at the bottom of a body of water) for our homework, even though I already have the answer. Kris is tall and thin and cute. He's also smart and has a great sense of humor. I wonder whether he has a girlfriend, so I ask Stacey. She settles the issue promptly, telling me to forget it; Kris Lim is going steady with Abby Barnett, a cheerleader.

Around the same time, I get an unexpected push out of my cage from Mom and Dad. The reason is Sam, now thirteen. They see her behaving like a typical teen, talking on the phone with girlfriends every night, hanging out on campus after school or at the mall on weekends. And they don't understand why I'm not doing these same things.

"Lauren is fifteen, how come she doesn't have friends? Why doesn't she ever leave the house?" they ask Waldy, of all people. I'm shocked when Waldy tells me about this conversation, aware that such questions could bring our secret that much closer to being found out.

"Don't worry," Waldy tells me later, when we're folding laundry. "I have a plan. We're going to get you a boyfriend."

"Get me what?"

"You'll pick out a boy or two, and we'll pretend one of them is your boyfriend."

"I still don't get it."

She pulls me into the corner of the laundry room and lowers her voice. "Listen, you dummy. You have to pretend, so Mom and Dad don't get suspicious about us. Don't worry, baby, it'll be fine."

To carry out her plan, Waldy suggests we look through my yearbook and find a suitable boyfriend.

I've gone halfway through the yearbook when she asks, "So who are you going to pick?" When I turn to look at her, she's got that sly smile that gives her lips an upward curl at each end.

"I don't know," I say. The process of searching for a boyfriend under Waldy's direction is unnerving for me, I suppose because I already sense we're at cross-purposes.

She takes the book from me and flips through the pages herself, stopping to point out a few candidates, asking me what I think of them. To each I shake my head or scrunch up my nose in distaste.

"There must be a boy," she says with a new note of annoyance.

"Well, there is one in my earth science class."

"Oh yeah. What's his name?

"Kris Lim."

She frowns. "What is he, Chinese?"

"Something Asian."

"Your father may not be crazy about that. But it doesn't matter. You're not going to do anything with this boy. He's just for show."

"The problem is he already has a girlfriend named Abby."

"Just get rid of her."

"What do you mean?"

"I'm sure you're smarter than Kris or Abby. Plant a doubt in his mind about her. It doesn't even have to be true. But make sure he likes you first."

I begin by waging a flirting campaign on Kris in earth science. Then I "let" him walk me to my next class. With some coaching from Waldy, I send him text messages constantly from home, pouring on the flattery. Boys are easy to win over, I discover. After a few more weeks of this, when I'm sure Kris is smitten with me, I make my move. I tell him that I have it on good authority that Abby cheated on him with a beefy halfback on the football team. I imply that they slept together. Well, that does it. After a few days of hemming and hawing, Kris breaks up with Abby and becomes my "boyfriend."

On our first date, Waldy, my mother and Chase drop me off at a Japanese restaurant called Oasis. Waldy is real quiet during the drive, and I notice she doesn't look at me when I get out of the car. Waiting for me at the curb is Kris. His parents are already seated inside the restaurant.

"Hey," he says, giving me a big smile, checking me out. "You look nice."

"Thanks," I say, glad I wore my new jeans and a belt that sparkles.

As the car pulls away, Chase yells, "Bye, have a good date" from the back seat.

"Who was that driving you?" Kris asks.

"Oh, that's Waldy. My little brother's nanny."

Once we're seated in a booth inside with Kris's parents, some "getting to know you" goes on. His dad is a doctor specializing in geriatrics. His mother, a nurse, works in his dad's clinic. After we order, Mrs. Lim quizzes me the way all mothers do, like we're in a job interview, asking how many brothers and sisters I have, what my dad does, what's our religion (they're Catholic, and a combination of Chinese and Filipino she tells me), whether my mom works, blah, blah, blah. Kris smiles at me a lot, but he and his father let Mrs. Lim do most of the talking.

When the food comes, I notice the three of them unwrapping the chopsticks sitting next to our plates.

"Do you know how to use chopsticks, Lauren?" Mrs. Lim asks.

"Sure," I say, picking them up. I've never actually eaten with chopsticks, but as stubborn as I am, I don't want to admit it.

Anyway, how hard can it be? So I watch Kris carefully and try to follow along. The teriyaki is simple enough to deal with, but forget the rice and noodles. I'm probably getting about 10 percent of the food I pick up with the chopsticks from the plate into my mouth. Finally, Dr. Lim, who's sitting next to me, reaches over and adjusts my fingers to the correct position on my chopsticks. He does it without saying a word. After that, I get about half of what I pick up with the chopsticks into my mouth.

"Thanks," I say, and everyone smiles politely, obviously relieved.

At last, dinner ends. His parents say goodbye and we're on our own. Next stop is the movies, where we settle into middle seats in a middle row. The lights go down and Brendan Fraser's face appears on screen, and that's my last memory of the film. By then, Kris is holding my hand, and the electricity that's been building up for weeks between us gets turned up to the maximum. It's fun to just feel it and not do anything much about it, as he moves his hand to my knee and then puts his arm on the back of my seat and plays with my hair. It takes nearly the whole movie before Kris turns my chin toward him and kisses me. We go from a light brushing of lips to a deep kiss, and stay that way. Don't ask me for how long.

This kiss, my first with a boy, is nothing short of a revelation to me. My distinct memory of what's going through my mind and body is *Oh my God, this is what I'm supposed to be doing!* I still get goose bumps when I think of it. The funniest thing is that we're still lost in that kiss when an usher shines his flashlight on us and says, "Hey, you gotta cool it or take it outside." We look around and see that people on all sides are staring at us with annoyed looks on their faces.

"Oh, sorry," I say.

Kris laughs, and so do I, but we behave ourselves after that, keeping it at hand-holding until the credits roll and we get up. We're still holding hands when we walk into the lobby. I remember the smile on Kris's face, and the amazing realization that comes to me. *I can have this. I can be normal. I don't have to live the way I have been.* I feel hopeful and absolutely wonderful. Unfortunately, my bliss doesn't last long.

When we reach the sidewalk under the movie marquee, there are two cars waiting: one driven by Kris's dad, the other with Waldy at the wheel, alone. She looks pissed.

"So I'll call you tomorrow," Kris is saying as I let go of his hand.

"Great," I answer, forcing a smile as I brace myself for the worst.

It doesn't happen that night. After a silent ride home, my parents are up when we get back and they want to hear how my date went. I linger with them, avoiding Waldy.

Waldy's retribution for my enjoying the date with Kris occurs on Monday night, when Mom and Dad are out, after Chase has gone to bed and Sam is safely behind a closed bedroom door. Waldy intercepts me when I'm brushing my teeth, already in my pajamas. When she grabs me by the arm, she has a look on her face that says "don't say a word," so I don't protest and let her drag me down the hall.

"What did I do?" I whine after she locks her bathroom door behind us. "You told me I had to get a boyfriend, so I did."

"You little sneak. You let him touch you, didn't you?!" And then she punches me in the stomach. When I cower on the floor, she kicks me so I fall over onto my side. "You're just a little whore, aren't you?" She grabs her hairbrush and whacks me on the back, buttocks, wherever she can reach that I can't cover with my arms.

"What else did you let him do? Come on, tell me!"

"Nothing. I did nothing."

She picks me up so she can stick her face right up to mine and says, "You're a liar. I know you kissed him. He felt you up too, didn't he?" And then she grabs my breast and squeezes it real hard, letting me know that it belongs to her, not some sixteen-year-old boy.

"No, he didn't," I say in protest.

"No? Why is that?" she asks, getting eerily calm. "Why didn't you put out for him? Is it because you love me?"

"Yes, I do."

"Then lean over and show me."

"What?"

"Just take off your pajama bottoms and stick your ass up in the air like you're a dog."

I do what I'm told, trying to stop my body from shaking.

"Yeah, just like that." And then, as I feared might happen someday, because of some scenes I saw on her porno tapes, she sticks first one finger and then two up into my anus. At first she can't get in very far, but she keeps at it, pushing and pushing. It hurts so bad, I cry out, which I immediately wish I hadn't done. She lays a punch into my side as a warning. When I'm quiet again, she changes her position so she can hold me in place with one knee on either side of my ass. Now I can't move at all. And that's when she puts something sharp into my anus. I see later that it was a fork. I feel like I'm being ripped open, and all I can do is hold my breath and count the bathroom tiles, a pattern of blue and tan squares that I had already gotten to know well from other times I spent on that floor, waiting for something to be over.

"Who do you belong to, my *bonita gringa?*" she whispers in my ear.

"You. I belong to you."

"*Cierto,*" she says. All I hear is her breathing hard, and then I see her clothes dropping onto the floor next to me. She's standing up, straddling my rear, one leg on each side as I feel some liquid dribbling on my butt. And that's when I realize she's peeing on me.

"There, now come to bed and be my good girl again," she says in a sickeningly sweet voice.

By then I can't get up, I hurt so bad, which she seems to understand, so she picks me up and carries me onto the bed like I'm a baby. I tremble for a long time as she rubs up against my back with her hips and stomach, and holds me there tightly.

Despite the awful price I had to pay for venturing emotionally away from Waldy, a part of me felt good about the fact that I was a little bit less her prisoner after that first date with Kris. She obviously detected what must have been written all over my face: my excitement about having this new relationship with a boy, and everything he represented. If only I'd had the courage right then to tell the truth to someone so I could have been safe from her. But that would have required turning over the only mother figure I had to the police. And I just couldn't do it. Not yet.

6

Sweet Sixteen

Spring, 2000

Getting my driver's license is the next big step in my process of getting free. After I get a car for my birthday, I take over Waldy's job of school chauffeur. Now I spend time with Kris after school, and decide whether the two of us will take Chase to Power Smoothie for shakes or just sit in the car and play the stereo. Then if Sam doesn't have another ride, I pick her up from practice before driving us all home.

My emotional dependency on Waldy is lessening as I come to care for and trust Kris. Ironically, when it comes to sex, he and I decide to wait until we're older or maybe even engaged before we go "all the way." I love dating him, and everything that goes with being courted and romanced. Whenever he kisses me, I feel he cares for me, but then it makes me sad when I contrast that with how dirty I feel when Waldy is done with me.

There are so many different versions of me it's hard to keep track of who I am at any given moment. There's daughter Lauren, then there's Kris's girlfriend Lauren and, of course, Waldy's sex slave and coconspirator in secrecy Lauren. But it's still complicated, because Waldy plays an even larger role in stabilizing our household as my mother's emotional state deteriorates. Chase, now ten, loves Waldy and depends on her more than ever. Even Sam, who regularly challenges Waldy's authority, would rather she not leave. I'm very aware, even during this confusing time, that if I turn on Waldy and tell my father even a fraction of what's going on, she'll be instantly fired, or worse. He could kill her and go to jail for the rest of his life. Where would that leave Chase, Samantha and me? We'd be without a mother surrogate or a father. So, in my admittedly skewed version of reality, I have to make this sacrifice for my sister and brother.

One morning before school, we're all in the kitchen when Sam asks Mom, who's sitting at one end of the breakfast counter, for the permission slip she gave her earlier in the week to sign. Sam needs it today so she can go on a class trip to Disney World. Mom has probably misplaced it, but instead of simply admitting that, she claims Sam never gave it to her.

Waldy, who's across the room making lunches, suggests that Mom check her purse to see if it's there.

"Who the hell do you think you are?" Mom screams at Waldy.

"I'm just trying to help you."

"I've had enough of your butting into things that are none of your damn business."

At that point, I want to get Chase, who's still eating his cereal at the table, out of there, so I pick up both of our backpacks. "Chase, Sam, we have to go or we'll be late," I say.

"No way," Sam protests, still standing at the other end of the breakfast counter opposite Mom. "I need my permission slip or I won't be able to go to Orlando."

"Isn't that a shame," Mom says in sarcastic sympathy as she takes the pen Sam gave her to sign with and throws it at her, grazing Sam's cheek.

"Ow," whines Sam, putting a hand on her face.

"It didn't even touch you," Mom says, now on her feet.

Perhaps thinking Mom is about to slap Sam, Waldy steps in between the two of them, saying to Mom simply, "Don't touch her."

"Get out of my way. That's it. I want you out of here. You're fired."

Silence follows as we stand frozen in place. The spell is broken when Mom knocks over her stool and storms out.

"She'll calm down," says Waldy, with a pat on Chase's head. "I'm driving her to her two o'clock doctor's appointment. She probably let her meds run out."

"Yeah. It doesn't look like she slept last night," I concur.

"So what about my permission slip?" Sam asks, single-minded as usual.

Waldy grabs a steno pad and pen from a drawer. "I'll write it out and Lauren can sign your mother's name. No one will notice."

"Fine with me," says Sam with her first smile of the morning.

Waldy prints out two lines of neat block lettering giving Sam permission to take the two-day trip by bus to Orlando with the rest of the seventh grade. Under it, I scrawl my best forged signature of "Mrs. Patricia Book" and hand the pad to Sam, who tears off the page and puts the folded slip in the pocket of her school uniform.

"Now go on. You're already late," Waldy says.

When Chase and I return home from school later that day, Mom and Waldy are both in the house and there's no visible strain beyond the usual.

Something else at this time adds to the chaos that comes into our household every spring when the legislature goes into session— the launch of the 2000 presidential election. The Florida primary in March takes over state politics, the same territory Dad covers as a lobbyist for many politicians and counties, so he's involved in all of it. Then if you recall what happens after the general election in November when the Florida recount begins, you'll understand why things only get and stay crazier until inauguration day, January 2001, just in time for the next legislative session. What this means for me is that Dad is twice as busy during the last year and a half of my abuse.

Thankfully, I have Kris. He becomes my new ally and, most important, someone who pushes me to say what I'm feeling, and why. He and I will be talking on the phone at night when Waldy gives me a look or pats me on the shoulder, telling me I need to go with her. To him I say "I have to go," and hang up abruptly. When he asks why I did that the next day, I tell him Mom wanted something or she was making a fuss, so I had to go deal with it. I can't yet bring myself to confess the real cause of my distress. I worry that Kris will find the truth so disgusting he'll reject me.

I've since learned that the emotional damage done to abused children can be mitigated if they have another trusted person in their lives who helps sustain them during the period of abuse. Often, it's a grandmother, an older sibling or friend. Even if you can't bring yourself to tell this person what's happening and who's hurting you, their presence still helps to keep your spirit alive because you just know that someone loves you. Kris does that for me, starting with our first date in the ninth grade until I finally come clean with the truth, and afterward.

My double life leaves me in a state of near-constant emotional confusion. It's like everything and everyone in my world (including me) are balanced on top of each other like a house of cards. If the wind blows too hard, we'll all collapse, and things that are barely hanging together will come apart. So I do everything I can to keep the wind still, including squashing my own feelings, along with any wants and desires I might have beyond the most basic.

In the deposition I give for Waldy's trial, the lawyer defending her keeps coming back to the major contradiction I was living at this time: how I could hate the abuse I received from her, but still love my abuser.

> *Q. You said you were forced on certain occasions to do these things.*
>
> *A. Correct.*
>
> *Q. You also said you never voluntarily did them. Right?*
>
> *A. Right.*
>
> *Q. Okay. But you told the police that you did love Waldina.*
>
> *A. Yes I did.*
>
> *Q. Can you describe for us what you meant by that description of your feelings for her?*
>
> *A. She made me feel safe. She protected me. She placed a wedge between my mother and me while she was there. And she filled that gap. She never let me get close to friends my age or my parents. She was it. And maybe back then I did confuse love with total power or fear. But that's what happened.*

The lawyer's next question addresses the period after I started dating Kris in the ninth grade, and what that changed for me.

A. I started to see things a little bit differently. I didn't really want to spend all my time in the house . . . I was tired of constantly lying to my parents.

Q. Why would you always have to be in the house?

A. Because Waldy was very controlling. And if she couldn't see me, she thought I was doing something wrong.

Q. Did you ever go to Mom and say "It's getting too strict for me"?

A. My parents wanted me to go out. It was Waldy not letting me go out.

Q. But she told you to go out with Kris Lim.

A. She told me to see him in school. And then I should just talk to my parents about him, as a cover-up.

Q. How many times did you lie to Waldy about where you were going in relationship to Kris Lim?

A. All the time.

Q. Did Waldina become jealous of him?

A. Yes, she did.

This is the craziness going on when I'm fifteen and sixteen years old. Very few people have any idea how bad a state my mother is in during this time. I'm dating Kris but lying to Waldy, so she doesn't freak out about my romance with him. And I'm still not telling anyone about my twisted relationship with her. Sometimes, it's hard to even remember what I've said to Dad, Mom, Waldy, Kris, Sam or Chase.

When my sophomore school year ends, we take a family vacation to San Francisco, where Dad has a sister and we have cousins with whom we usually have a lot of fun. Per our custom, Waldy comes along for the week, sharing a hotel room with the three of us. My chief memory of that trip is the humiliation and fear of being found out in that hotel room. When Waldy insists on having sex under the covers of our bed, we're just feet away from Sam and Chase.

Fall, 2000

If things are barely holding together up to this point, they start to unravel when tenth grade begins. It's so bad that Dad, who's tied up with the presidential election, realizes something has to change. He and Mom fight constantly. Judging by the noise level, they may finally get a divorce. Later, I find out that, starting that fall, Waldy had been making tape recordings of our family's fights whenever she could get close enough with her small recorder. Since Mom and Sam were also fighting a lot, she taped some of their nasty arguments, too. The existence of these tapes eventually becomes a factor in her legal battle. Apparently, she thought they offered her some sort of ammunition for blackmailing my parents. She was clever enough to see that I was moving away from her total control, and no doubt had begun to think she might need some kind of personal protection.

As for me, the stress of keeping up so many competing roles starts to show. By October, I'm losing weight, down from 110 to ninety pounds. I burst into tears without an ostensible "reason," although the cause is usually some pressure from Waldy to service her sexual demands. When Mom or Dad ask me what's wrong, I lie, saying it's the pressure of keeping my grades up, the SATs later that month or some term-paper deadline.

This is when Dad brings in a family therapist—actually two of them—to try and help us kids cope with the situation at home. One, Dr. Levin, sees Chase and me, separately, once a week. Another woman therapist from the same practice sees Sam separately, also once a week. Then Dr. Levin sees Mom and Dad together, not to save their marriage, Dad explains to me later, but to help them improve how they deal with each other in front of us kids, to make things calmer at home. I don't know about Chase or Sam, but the problem for me in therapy is that I'm so used to lying, I find it pretty simple to fool Dr. Levin. When I say it's the stress of grades getting me down and making me not eat, he buys those reasons, and that's what we talk about. I'm sort of amazed that he can't tell there's much more than that going on. Isn't that what therapists are supposed to be so good at?

The person who I'm least able to fool that year is Kris.

One Saturday afternoon, we're in his family room playing cards, my favorite game, blackjack, and I'm winning. His parents keep their house much warmer than ours; they use ceiling fans at times when we have our air conditioning on. So I take off my sweatshirt and have only a loose halter top on. While we're playing, Kris doesn't realize that from where I'm sitting on the sofa I can see his cards, so I'm basically cheating. Finally, after something like my eighth straight win, he catches on and comes after me using a kind of playful wrestling hold. He grabs my arms and turns me over on the sofa. This turns my top inside out and exposes my lower back. He stops.

"How'd you get these bruises?" he asks, first touching my back and then letting me go and sitting back down on the sofa next to me. When I look at him, he's frowning. It isn't the first time he's asked me about a black and blue mark or a sore limb.

"Oh, I fell in the shower."

He raises his eyebrows and licks his lips, seemingly disappointed by my answer. It's clear to me that he isn't buying it.

"Lauren, what's going on?"

"Nothing."

"Come on, I care about you. You always blame your mother when you're upset. But she doesn't hit you. Neither does your father. Who does that leave?"

I look away, feeling caught and afraid.

"It's Waldy, isn't it?"

"Yeah." Confronted like that, I decide to leave the sexual abuse out of my confession. "She hits me sometimes."

"Why do you and your parents put up with that?"

"They don't know. It's not so bad, Kris."

"It's downright weird is what it is. I know Waldy doesn't like me. It's like I'm taking you away from her or something. It's just not normal. Why does she care?"

"Well, nothing's normal at our house. Let's just drop it, okay?"

He shakes his head, saying, "All right. But I better not see any more bruises on you."

The weirdness Kris is referring to is Waldy's blatant attempts to ruin our relationship. One Friday night, he and I are at our house after a movie date. Waldy comes in to the kitchen where we're having a snack. After hello, she goes right to "Oh, a boy named Jason called and said he'd pick you up at six tomorrow." She knows there's a Jason in my class who I did a school project with, so we had to talk on the phone once or twice, but she's well aware that there's nothing more to it than that. She's just trying to upset Kris. Pretty transparent, but it adds to the weirdness factor that is now getting to Kris and making him increasingly suspicious.

April, 2001

We've come to the day I call Black Monday, the culmination of the bad things that have been building up for years in our household. It starts the Sunday night before, with Mom going into

Sam's room while she's asleep to chastise her for something. Sam wakes up pissed off and tells Mom to get out of her room. In the process of Sam slamming the door on her, Mom collides with a shelf and knocks something heavy onto Sam's head. By the next day, Sam has a black eye. In the morning, their tussle escalates. Mom tells Sam the black eye is her own fault and goes after her, smacking Sam across the face. Sam hits back, and it takes Waldy to separate them. Then Mom goes after Waldy, but Waldy is much stronger than she is, so she manages to restrain her. Mom pulls away from Waldy's hold and tells her she's fired—again. But this time Mom escorts Waldy to the door and tells her never to come back.

That leaves us alone with an out-of-control Mom. She and Sam are still at it, yelling and threatening each other. Chase is so freaked out, he's got his head in the clothes dryer in order to get away from their yelling and screaming. I can hear him talking to himself saying, "Stop yelling, please" and "I want Waldy back."

I can see this going from terrible to worse. I call Dad in Tallahassee and tell him what's going on. "I told you," I say to him, barely able to talk because I'm coughing and crying. "I told you this would happen. You've got to do something, right now!"

"I'm sorry. Calm down, Lauren," he says. "I'll call Dr. Levin and see if he can get to the house."

When Dr. Levin (because he was our family therapist and the person to whom I finally reveal my abuse) is called in to give a deposition for Waldy's trial, this is how he describes what occurred on Black Monday, when he gets to the house in response to Dad's call.

Dr. Levin: Pat was very agitated. She was pacing back and forth, and I had some trouble getting her to calm down. I was on the phone with Ron and telling him I didn't think it was safe for the kids to be in the home with her, alone without Waldy being there. So Ron agreed to that and said he would make arrangements to get a plane chartered and a limo to pick up the kids.

Then the lawyer asks Dr. Levin about Mom's reaction to Dad making this plan.

Dr. Levin: She wasn't happy about it. She asked me to leave. I said I wanted to wait for the limo to arrive, but she opened the front door and told me to get out.

Since Waldy's lawyer wants to get Dr. Levin to talk about Waldy's positive contributions to the household, he asks Levin what, if anything, we kids had ever told him in therapy about Waldy, prior to the accusations of sexual assault I made against her.

Dr. Levin: Waldy was the stabilizing force in the home. Since Ron was more often working late or in Tallahassee, and Pat was too emotionally unstable to provide the mothering for the children, Waldy was really the mother surrogate for the kids.

After Dr. Levin has come and gone from our house on Black Monday, the limo that is supposed to transport us to the airport has still not arrived. After I lock Chase in our car, I return to the living room to find Mom screaming at Sam, poking her in the same black eye that she gave her the night before. Sam, at this point, appears to be passed out on the sofa, like she can't take it anymore. I know I have to separate them, so I wake up Sam and drag her stumbling out to the car to wait there with Chase. This takes about fifteen minutes. With the two of them now safe, I go sit on the front steps to watch for the limo. When it finally pulls up and it's time to go, I have a bad feeling about leaving Mom alone in the house. So I tell the limo driver to get Sam and Chase from my car while I go back in. In the foyer I see a trail of blood. And then I find Mom on the living room sofa covered in more blood. It looks like she just slit her wrist.

Most people seeing this scene would call 911, but I don't. The reason relates to everything I've been telling you about my family. There have been so many incidents, primarily having to do with my mom, that I've learned we don't call the police or paramedics unless it's absolutely necessary. We keep private things private. Now I see that Mom is conscious, although dazed and upset.

"Mom, you need to go to the emergency room."

"No. It's nothing. And don't you dare call anyone."

I feel bad and worried about her, but there's nothing else I can do. It feels as if Sam and Chase and I are in some kind of emergency evacuation, and there's no time to waste. When I say goodbye to my mother and shut the front door of our house behind me, I'm crying so hard I can hardly walk straight.

The next thing I remember is the limo pulling onto the tarmac of Fort Lauderdale Executive Airport and depositing us next to a chartered Lear jet. We land in Tallahassee where Dad meets us, and we go straight to his hotel where we spend the next two weeks.

The next day, Dr. Levin goes back to the house to check on Mom. He calls to tell us she's still very upset about the events of the day before. And she has a bandage on her wrist. When he asks her about it, Mom says she cut herself accidentally while trying to restrain Samantha. Of course, I'd seen Mom before and after Sam left the house, so I knew the blood had nothing to do with my sister.

Mom later tells me that she hit her wrist on the corner of the table, slicing it open by accident just before she left. When we return from Tallahassee, Waldy is back at the house, no longer fired.

After Black Monday, it's hard to pretend anything in our house is normal, or even okay. It's as if we all know there's another shoe (or shoes) about to drop; we just don't know exactly which one and when.

7

Freedom and Fallout

June, 2001

The events I share in this chapter are vividly etched in my memory. In addition, many are documented in legal depositions—mine and those of my father, mother and Dr. Levin—as well as in other official court proceedings.

Early in the summer, our family moves from the house where we've always lived in Aventura (north Miami) about thirty miles north to a new, larger one in Plantation (Fort Lauderdale area), which is nearer to school and farther from Dad's office. Unlike the Aventura house, our home in Plantation has two levels with marble stairs leading from the upstairs family bedrooms down to the kitchen, living area and Waldy's quarters.

It's the summer before my junior year and I have a job working for the Broward County Homeless Assistance Center, where I help prepare lunch for hundreds of people who go there every day for a hot meal. Kris works part time in his parents' geriatric medicine clinic. We see each other several times a week and talk on the phone often. Like any girl in her first serious relationship, I do a lot of fantasizing about what my life will be like if I marry this boy. In the privacy of my bedroom (for the first time, I have my own room), I draw hearts and paste snapshots of Kris and me inside them, captioned with his name and mine, as "Mrs. Lauren Lim."

With the hectic schedule of moving and starting my summer job, I've managed to avoid Waldy, and it's been months since she's coerced me into having sex with her. I know she's unhappy about it, but I've managed to stay busy and far enough away to escape her wrath. Lately, she's been trying sweetness to get me back under her control. She'll be very nice and friendly when she first sees me in the morning, asking if I need help with my hair. After work, she'll ask me if I want a snack. When I say I'm going out again, she'll pout and sigh. Since I'm up and out of the house by six-thirty, I usually go to bed early, by nine. I'll say goodnight and lock my bedroom door. Then the next time I see her she'll be curt. Her volatility and the possibility that she'll lash out at me is always a concern in the back of my mind.

All summer I'm hoping she'll just let go and move on, and not make it necessary for me to tell anyone about what she's been doing to me for all these years. With college plans and envisioning a life away from home, I see the light at the end of the tunnel, but I'm not sure how it will all end. I'm brainwashed enough by Waldy to think of "our relationship" as something I am in by choice. I don't understand that I'm still a deluded child under the control of a sociopath. It's what happens to abused kids. We develop a defensive need (a false belief) that we can control everything in our lives; that is, except the person who's abusing us. So in my mind I believe I can avoid nasty revelations or anyone calling the police—and, of course, the shame for me and embarrassment for my parents that would be certain to result from people finding out. It's pretty naive of me to think all this bad stuff will just go away, but that's still the brainwashed girl I am at sixteen, after nearly four years of abuse.

July, 2001

Since I leave work right after we clean up from lunch, I'm usually the first one home. Chase goes to and from day camp on a bus, and Sam is in an all-day sports program.

One afternoon, I come home to find my room vandalized. The hearts with photos of me and Kris that I've been keeping in my desk drawer are torn up and thrown all over my bedroom floor. I know it's just me and Waldy home right now, and I'm really upset at what she's done. So I call her from the top of the stairs. When she comes I accuse her of ruining my things, but she denies doing it, saying it must have been Mom or Sam. I know she's lying, and say so. But instead of getting defensive, she takes the opposite tack and pours on the sweetness.

"Don't talk like that. I've really missed you, baby," she says, putting her hand gently on my forearm. "Let's spend some time together."

"I can't. I'm too tired."

"I just want to make you feel good, like I used to, when you were just my little *gringa* and I was your Waldy."

I say nothing and stand there without moving.

"Come with me," she commands, her tone now steely.

"No," I say as I turn to face her. "No more." My chest is so tight I can barely breathe. I'm feeling emboldened but terrified at the same time, and desperate not to show my fear.

"Don't be like that," she coerces as she pulls me into the hallway, near the top of the stairs. My bedroom is the closest.

"What are you doing?" I ask, turning to face her with my back to the stairs.

"I've got things set up for us in my room."

"I said no, I'm not coming." Then I yank my arm away from her. She pushes me either in anger or by accident, and I fall backward, tumbling down the stairs. I try to stop myself but I can't; the momentum is too much. Not even the narrow landing stops me. As I hit the marble floor of the foyer headfirst, I feel a sharp pain in my neck and cry out. When I open my eyes, the room looks blurry. I moan and turn over, waiting for my vision to come back. When it does, I see Waldy walking down the stairs toward me. But instead of stopping, she steps right over me saying, "You better get up." I hear her walk down the hall and into her room, and then the sound of her TV turned up loud.

I'm relieved she's gone, but too weak to stand. I drag myself to the living room sofa and climb onto it, curling into a fetal position. I know no one can hear me crying. My wracking sobs make the pain in my neck sting even more. It feels like I'm crying years' worth of tears.

At some point the crying stops, but when I open my eyes the reality of what just happened and my totally screwed-up life come back, bringing a feeling of hopelessness so overwhelming that it's like someone just put a hundred-pound weight on my chest. I'm afraid that I'll never have the love I crave, because it will always be like this. It's as if everything is closing in on me, especially the walls I've erected to keep anyone from seeing this part of me: the helpless baby who cries when she feels pain, and wants nothing more than to have her mommy hold her and protect her from getting hurt again.

In my mind's eye, I see two roads stretching out in front of me. One is dark and familiar; it's my life as it's always been. The other, shrouded in fog and hard to see, promises light and love, but feels risky since it's unknown. On some level, I know I'm facing the choice whether to live or die. For several moments, I drift down the dark road and consider ending my life. I even figure out how I'll do it. There are plenty of pills in Mom's medicine cabinet. If I take enough, I'm sure they'll do the trick.

But then I turn back to the direction where I started, and I see Chase's face; he's crying because he thinks I'm gone for good. Dad is there, too; worried, waiting. When I inch back further, I see Kris standing off to the side, already headed down the new road. That's when my choices become crystal clear: in order to live, I have to let someone help me. I understand that the person who's closest to me now, Kris, is the one in the position to extend a lifeline, but for me to reach it, I'll have to show him exactly where I am, which means I have to tell the whole truth.

By the time anyone else in the family gets home that day, I'm sore but walking again. Nobody notices my sad and withdrawn mood as anything out of the ordinary.

August, 2001

It takes me a few more weeks to muster the courage, but one morning, while I'm on a break at work, I call Kris at home. I'm determined to finally give him a truthful answer to the question he's asked many times that summer: "What's wrong, Lauren?"

When Kris answers his phone, I speak in short, clipped phrases, not our usual easy banter. I say I have to tell him something, but I can't say it on the phone. I'll need to meet him later. He understands I'm very upset and keeps asking what's wrong. I hear a lot of shouting on his TV in the background.

"Is it your mom again?" he asks.

"No. She's the same."

"Did Sam get in trouble?"

"No."

"Okay, then it's Waldy, isn't it?"

"Yes."

"Did she hit you again?"

"No, that's not it."

"What did she do to you?"

There's a long silence. Later Kris tells me that the truth comes to him as he waits for me to answer. Oddly, he's helped by the *Jerry Springer Show* on his TV. There's a family on screen dealing with the aftermath of an incest charge.

"She sexually abused you?" It's as much a statement as it is a question.

"Yes, and it's been going on for years."

"Oh Jesus, that's awful . . ." After a long silence, Kris says, "You've got to tell your father, today."

"I know I do," I say. The relief of finally telling someone is quickly followed by a feeling of panic about what's going to happen next.

Kris and I agree to meet later that afternoon at his house, since we know we'll be alone there. So I'm surprised and perplexed when he shows up at the homeless center before I leave work.

"Why are you here?" I ask.

"Guess who called me right after we talked and demanded I meet her?"

"Waldy," I say with a sinking feeling in my stomach.

"Yeah. And you're not going to believe what she said to me."

"You met her?"

"Yeah . . . just now at Power Smoothie."

"What did she say?"

"She said, 'You're not going to date Lauren anymore. Leave her alone or I'll kill you.'"

"Oh my God. Kris, she's capable of doing it."

"Nah. She's all talk."

"You don't know her like I do."

"Listen, I'm not worried about me right now. You have to report her."

"I will. I promise."

"When?"

"I don't know."

"Lauren, if you don't do it, I'll call your father myself."

"No, let me. I have a one o'clock appointment with Dr. Levin. I'll tell him first. I promise I'll do it."

"Everything will be okay. Don't forget I'm here for you."

As he holds me, I try to soak in some of his confidence that the future will be okay. But it's hard to think past today and what I've still got in front of me. On my drive home, where I'm going to stop briefly to change clothes, I keep reminding myself that I just have to get through tonight. By tomorrow it will all be over and I'll be free.

When I walk into the kitchen, Waldy is there to greet me. "Hey, baby," she says. "I've been waiting to talk to you. I've got a surprise."

Oh no, I think. *Doesn't she know Kris would have told me what she said to him?*

Apparently not.

"Come with me. There's something I have to show you," she continues.

"Show me right here," I say as we stand alone in the kitchen.

"All right," she replies with a little childlike smile on her face. And then out of her shirt pocket she pulls a ring. It's a silver band with some kind of rhinestone-like stone on it, the kind you buy at Walmart, not Macy's.

"What is that?"

"It's an engagement ring for you."

"Oh." I'm speechless. It's as if I'm being sucked into some kind of black hole from which I'll never be able to escape.

"Will you marry me?" she asks me in a dead serious tone.

"Waldy, it's not possible. Besides, I'm seeing Kris."

"No you're not. He's gone now. Your life is with me. I've got it all planned out. You'll get your money and we'll go to Honduras, to the mountains where I know people. We'll start our own coffee ranch."

I look at the imploring expression on her face and know it would be dangerous for me to let on any of my real thoughts or feelings. I'll have to play along for the time being.

"I can't really talk about this now," I say. "I've got to go see Dr. Levin now. Can we talk about it more tomorrow?"

"Sure, baby, but take this." And she hands me the ring.

"Okay," I say, holding the ring in my palm. My fear has transformed into a wave of pity for her. Maybe she mistakes it for some other more positive feeling welling up inside me. She puts her arms around me and hugs me tight, making me cringe.

"I'm sorry, I have to go," I say. "We'll talk more tomorrow."

When I walk into Dr. Levin's therapy office a little while later, it's like I'm on a high diving board; below me, a tiny pool of water.

When I look over the edge, I'm dizzy and disoriented. *Am I really going to do this?*

"Lauren, how are you today?" he asks.

What an absurd question, I think. The words come out of my mouth in an equally absurd jumble. "I'm fine. I mean I'm all right. But there's something you need to know. There's been a relationship between me and Waldy for years. I need your help to get out of it."

He asks only a few questions.

"Is there anything inappropriate about this relationship?"

"Yeah."

"Did it involve sexual contact?"

"Yes."

"Does anyone else know?

"Kris."

"Where is Waldy now?"

"At home."

"Do you feel in any immediate danger?"

"No."

"Look," I say to Dr. Levin, "I don't want you to tell my parents. I just need to get out of the relationship with her." I show him the ring Waldy gave me. "Look at this! She wants us to get married and run away together. Just tell me how you're going to help me get her away from me!"

My answers reveal that I'm still operating under the delusion that I have some control over my situation. Like I can get things to turn out the way I want them to, namely getting Waldy out of my life quietly, without hurting her or doing what the law requires.

"Lauren, I have the legal obligation to report any form of child abuse to social services and law enforcement within forty-eight hours," he says.

"Oh," I say quietly, withdrawing my legs into the chair and wrapping my arms around my chest. *Child abuse. Is that really what my relationship with Waldy amounts to?* "I didn't know that you had to report it."

"Yes, it's the law," he repeats.

We discuss again whether I feel in any immediate danger. I say no. I can put Waldy off for one more day. *After all, she wants me to freakin' marry her. She's not going to try anything nasty tonight.*

"I'm also going to have to speak to your father immediately, Lauren," Dr. Levin says, and I begin to understand that this situation has just taken on its own momentum.

"Okay."

"I want you to come back here early tomorrow morning so we can tell him together. Here's my private line," he says, handing me a business card with another number scribbled in pencil. "Call me if anything worrisome should occur in the next few hours."

You may wonder why I don't provide details to Dr. Levin when he asks me point-blank whether there's anything inappropriate about my relationship with Waldy. For one thing, I'm really embarrassed. But I'm also scared of what Waldy might do to me or Chase or even to Mom and Dad when she finds out that I've reported her. After keeping this secret for so long, it's terrifying to be saying even this much to anyone. I have no memory of the rest of the day or night.

Dad was about to board a plane to Tampa for an afternoon meeting when Dr. Levin called him, right after I left his office. Later when I hear Dad's description of the call, it's almost funny. Levin asks Dad when is the soonest he can meet in person to discuss a serious matter concerning me.

Upon hearing the words "serious matter," Dad goes through the litany of usual worst things on the list of every parent's worst nightmares: "Is she pregnant?" "Is she drinking?" "Is it drugs?" "Is she failing school?"

When Dr. Levin says no to each possibility, an exasperated Dad demands to know exactly what the problem is. But Dr. Levin says he can't tell him over the phone. When Dad asks whether he should board his plane, because he'll cancel the trip and come directly there if I am in some immediate danger, Dr. Levin assures him it can wait until the following morning, and that I'm not in danger.

So Dad goes to Tampa and returns that night, with a plan to meet me at Dr. Levin's office at seven o'clock the next morning. And because he doesn't yet know the nature of "the problem," Dad doesn't speak to me about it after he gets home late or before he leaves early the next morning, thinking he should hear whatever it is in the presence of Dr. Levin, as agreed.

The next morning, I'm awake but still in bed and dreading the day when Waldy knocks on my door. "Time to get up, baby." Although my alarm goes off at five-thirty, Waldy still makes it a point to come and knock shortly after that, like she's my personal snooze button. My hands are shaking while I drink a glass of orange juice in the kitchen. Waldy comes in and tells me she's going to drive Mom to her psychiatrist's office around noon, so she'll see me after work. My last sight of Waldy as a free woman, she's in her pajamas, walking our dog down the driveway. She waves goodbye as I drive away from the curb.

In the hallway outside Dr. Levin's office, I stop short, startled by the sound of a man's wailing. When I knock and the doctor lets me in, I see Dad, his face wet with tears, struggling to hold back his sobs. "Oh my God, Lauren, how did I miss this horrible thing in our own house? I'm so sorry, pipper. I'm so sorry."

I go to him and we hug, both of us crying.

After several minutes of him expressing his horror and remorse, asking me if I'm all right, and his reassurance that of course he believes me, Dad and Dr. Levin move into crisis management mode. When I tell him that Waldy will be driving Mom to her psychiatrist's office, Dad decides he can't tell Mom what's happened, at least not yet, since her reaction is too unpredictable. He and Dr. Levin agree that the priority is to get Waldy out of our house. Dr. Levin makes the point that immediately afterward Dad must call the sheriff to report Waldy's crime, since as a psychologist he's obliged by law to report any evidence of child sexual abuse (if Dad doesn't) and he could get in legal trouble if he fails to do so within forty-eight hours.

Remembering that Chase and Sam were planning to skip camp that day and hang out at home, Dad calls to say they both need to go to camp, no questions asked. Then he drives to Mom's doctor's office, where he phones Waldy from the car to say he has something he needs to give her; that she should leave Mom's keys with the receptionist and come down to meet him outside the building. As soon as Waldy gets in the car, he speeds off. Later I hear what went down between them in the car.

"What is it?" Waldy asks, clearly alarmed. "Why are you here?"

"I think you know damn well what's going on," he responds.

"Did Lauren say something about me?"

"Yes, she told me everything."

"She's lying. Lauren is a liar. You can't believe anything she says."

At which point Dad gets so angry he has a hard time controlling himself when he answers her, saying simply, "I don't think so. Waldy, it's over. You're getting the hell out of my house." He drives there and waits for her to pack her bag. Then he drops her off at a gas station and says she should never show her face to him or his children again.

Dad calls the sheriff soon after dropping Waldy off, and files a police report. A few hours later, Detective Juanita Reid comes to our home to interview me. Because she handles rape and children's sex abuse cases every day, and because she's a truly sensitive and caring person, Detective Reid is the first person who is able to get at the truth behind my vague statements. When I repeat what I said to Dr. Levin, that Waldy and I have had a relationship for years, Detective Reid gets right to the point.

"Lauren, when you say 'relationship,' do you mean that Waldy touched your vagina and other private parts of your body and made you touch hers?"

"Yes."

"Did she start doing this to you as soon as she became your nanny, when you were thirteen years old?"

"Yes."

"Where in your house did these activities occur?"

"Mostly in Waldy's bedroom and her bathroom, and then sometimes in my bedroom, and other times when we were on vacation in hotel rooms."

"Did she ever hit you or otherwise cause you to receive a bruise?"

"Yes."

"Did she threaten to harm you if you told your parents?"

"Yes."

Finally, the truth was out.

The sheriff also searches our whole house for evidence, taking "love notes" Waldy has written to me and notes I had written back to her, along with porno tapes they find in her room. That is the only physical evidence to support my charges against Waldy. Unlike some incest and sexual predator cases, there can be no "rape kit" to help prove the crimes committed. The rest of the case will have to be built on testimony by me and other family members. Of course, the immediate challenge for the sheriff is to find and arrest Waldy.

At this point, in August of 2001, the only people outside of law enforcement who know what has happened are my family, Kris and Dr. Levin, along with a handful of other psychotherapists and counselors I consult for emotional help. This will change in three months when Waldy is arrested in Oklahoma and brought back to Florida to face charges. But for now, I'm in a strange limbo: ostensibly safe, but crumbling from fear nonetheless.

For the first two weeks after Waldy is gone, I don't leave the house at all because I'm terrified that she's out there, lurking in the neighborhood. I keep imagining the horrible things she'll do to me in retribution for telling on her. I remember one night I'm sitting in the kitchen, holding a heating pad against my stomach. The temperature of the pad is up so high it's burning me. But I can't make myself turn it down or take it off my stomach. It must sound strange, but I need to have that burning feeling against my skin so I'll know I'm still there and alive.

I think we must have just had dinner. Mom and Dad, Chase and Sam are hanging around in the kitchen with me, everyone doing their best to act normal while I finish another crying jag.

"But what if she sneaks back and comes after me?" I ask, unable to get that picture out of my head.

"She's not coming back here, ever," Dad says emphatically.

"Pipsqueak, you don't have to worry about that. I took her keys and, anyway, the police are watching for her."

"She'll hide in the yard until she see's that I'm alone. You won't know she's there until it's too late."

I remember the look on Dad's face as he stood at the kitchen counter, not knowing what else to say to reassure me. "That's not going to happen," he finally says, although he seems to now be getting that words alone aren't working to calm me down.

Then I have an idea. "I know what we can do," I say. "If we put newspapers on the windows, she won't be able to see in."

"You can't be serious," Mom says, staring at me like I'm crazy.

"Please! Just do it," I cry out as tears fall down my face.

"I'll get the newspapers," says Dad.

"Okay, okay," Mom says. "Sam, get up and help me, please."

"Help you do what?!" Sam asks, confused.

"Get the tape and scissors out of the drawer in the pantry and bring them in here."

Sam makes no further protests as she does what she's told. When Dad gets back with a pile of newspapers, Sam separates out single sheets, applying a piece of tape to each of its corners before handing the sheet to Mom for hanging.

When all the windows in the back of the house are covered with newspaper, I feel less visible, and thus safer.

October 1, 2001

It's been six weeks since I reported my abuser, three weeks since 9/11 and two nights since I last slept. My weight is down to eighty-five pounds, from one hundred where it was in July. But that was already below my normal weight of 114, although I couldn't tell you the last time my weight or anything else in my life was "normal."

At home, we're all still shell-shocked. I think Mom and Sam might be feeling vindicated, since both had said for a long time that at the very least Waldy had overstepped her job description as a nanny. Exactly how far off the rails she went with me for so long is something we rarely address head-on. Instead, everyone walks on eggshells around me, jumping when I jump, becoming sad and helpless when I burst into tears and otherwise feeling confused and uncomfortable a great deal of the time.

This delayed reaction on my part, falling apart after my abuser is gone, is typical for anyone suffering from posttraumatic stress disorder, or PTSD. It's medically defined as a disorder associated with soldiers returning from war or with survivors of natural disasters and genocide, like the Holocaust or the war in Rwanda. But the same symptoms affect survivors of sexual or physical abuse, especially kids.

For me, once Waldy is gone from my life, the worst symptoms I experience are an inability to sleep, zero appetite, a tendency to be startled and cry and depression. Oh, and my hair starts to falls out, too . . . *what a drag.*

After Dr. Levin says that my situation goes "beyond his clinical experience," he recommends that I try two other psychologists in private practice who specialize in adolescents. But after trying both, and then five others who come highly recommended, I don't feel as though I am being understood by anyone, and decline to continue in therapy. Fortunately, Detective Reid, when she sees the poor shape I'm in, recommends I go to the Broward County Sexual Assault Treatment Center for psychological counseling.

Dad is reluctant, saying that since he has the means to pay for private care, shouldn't we be leaving county services to those who don't? Detective Reid points out that the center specializes in sex crimes against adults and children. There I'll get exactly the kind of treatment I need. Boy, is she ever right about that. Working with my new counselor, Mandy Wells, I feel seen, heard and understood for the first time.

I ended up working with Mandy at the center for two years, and I credit her and the rest of the staff with getting me through the most difficult part of my recovery. Since that time, Dad and I have worked to secure better funding for all of Florida's rape and sexual assault centers, so they can serve the thousands of women, men and children of both sexes who come to their doors each year in need of the same treatment I received nearly a decade ago. Until we helped get their funding made into a line item in Florida's annual budget and established a state trust fund—funded by the fines paid by sex offenders and certain other convicted criminals—these treatment centers were closing all over the state, leaving rape and sexual abuse victims without help just when they desperately needed it.

So what else am I doing during those three bizarre months, the interlude between nobody knowing and seemingly the whole world finding out about the worst thing that has ever happened to me? Mainly, I go to school. I come home. And I talk with Kris on the phone. I do some other, stranger things, too. When I manage to sleep at all, it's during daylight hours and only in Waldy's old bedroom. Why there? Believe me, my parents worry and quiz me about it. Does this mean I miss Waldy? No, I don't think it's that simple, I try to explain. It's more like a reasserting of control on my part: to be at the scene of the crime and be in charge of that physical space and my body in it for the first time. Now I can lie in that bed and sit on the carpet watching TV without anyone else being able to tell me what to do. The same goes for my not eating, although my problems with food would soon become dire and demand medical attention.

Sexually abused kids very often develop the eating disorders anorexia and bulimia during their abuse, or after it ends. The totally illogical reasoning from the point of view of the kid starving herself (and most often it is girls) is that after not having control over your body for so long, the act of deciding to eat or denying yourself food is the most overt way to regain that control. Of course, since this is all happening on a subconscious level, the anorexic girl has little real control.

When I get down to eighty pounds, Mandy raises the red flag. Although we'd been working on my not eating in therapy, I am not able to change this behavior, at least not in time to stop my rapid physical decline. At the worst point, I'm in danger of having my organs shut down. In another couple of weeks I would be dead. That's what Mandy tells me and Mom and Dad, saying I am too sick to continue working on the abuse alone. The clinical protocol that has to be followed, she explains, is to put me into intensive inpatient treatment for anorexia. This is done on two occasions during those six months. I hate being there, so each time I convince my doctors and parents that I can continue my therapy as an outpatient. It's very touch and go for a lot of that time until I get past the worst of my anorexia.

The person who surprised us by rising to the occasion and helping me most at home was my mother. She drove me back and forth to my outpatient therapy appointments and acted as my "food coach" at home. One night I was lying in bed in my room, sleeping fitfully, when I became aware of being watched. It freaked me out. I wasn't sure if I was having a flashback or a nightmare; both were common then. But when my eyes adjusted to the dark, I made out my mom standing very still in the middle of the room, watching me. I didn't move or say anything for several seconds. It was so strange and unlike her. Finally I asked, "What are you doing, Mom?"

"I'm just making sure you're still breathing," she said.

"Yeah . . . I am."

"I'm sorry I woke you up."

"That's okay."

"Do you need anything, water or another cover?"

"No, I'm good."

"All right. Sleep tight," she said. And then she left my room.

That's when I understood that my mother really had always cared about me, as she clearly did now. She had shown her love in the ways she was capable, all the while struggling with her own emotional problems.

On the nights I couldn't sleep, after it became clear there was no talking me into going to bed, Mom and Dad started coming up with things for me to do. It was like "get Lauren a hobby" time. Mom brought home knitting and ceramics kits, which I tried and actually liked. Although most nights when I couldn't sleep during those months what I did was bake desserts; kind of ironic since I never ate what I made.

The weirdest hours I spent during those months while Waldy was "on the run" occurred when Detective Reid asked me to come down to the police station to place calls to Waldy's cell phone. The idea was to get Waldy to speak about the sex acts she'd engaged in with me. *Pretty unlikely,* I thought, but under pressure agreed to go through with the ruse. They would give me things to say, like "But what about the things we did in your room? Were those things wrong?"

Why they thought this pedophile who had been crafty enough to get away with her crimes in my parents' house for the last four years was just going to start chatting about them on the phone, I'll never know. I guess it was worth a try.

But instead of incriminating herself, Waldy told me how much she loved and missed me and how she didn't hold what I did against me, while police and Detective Reid listened in and recorded our conversations. Pretty darn weird.

From the reports provided by the private detective Dad had hired, the sheriff knew exactly where Waldy was living during this time: at the home of her friend Carla in Oklahoma City. And that's exactly where the Oklahoma City police arrested her two weeks before Thanksgiving, after the Broward County sheriff insisted they take action. Oklahoma City arrested her pursuant to the Florida arrest warrant and held her without bail pending her extradition to Florida. It was Detective Reid who personally brought Waldy back to Fort Lauderdale and who, after two days of questioning, even got her to admit to her guilt, although Waldy later recanted this confession. It was a week after Thanksgiving 2001, when Waldy's presence in the Broward County jail and the charges against her were made public, generating a media firestorm.

8

Under the Law

November 29, 2001

The house phone rings while Mom, Sam, Chase and I are in the kitchen eating an early dinner. I should say I'm mostly moving the food around on my plate. It's been another stressful day awaiting legal developments. After she picks up the receiver, Mom's expression is dead serious. As she listens, the rest of us watch in silence. After hanging up, Mom delivers the news in a controlled voice, quoting Dad verbatim.

"Dad says that on her first appearance in court, Waldy was not granted a bond and so she was held for formal arraignment at a later date."

"What does that mean again?" I ask, forgetting how Dad had explained it this morning before he left for the court hearing.

"It means Waldy will be held over for trial in jail without bail."

Sam and Chase both turn their heads to stare at me. My jaw drops as the weight of what I've just heard sinks in. It's hard to imagine Waldy behind bars. Apparently, I'm not the only one who's having trouble picturing it.

"Does that mean she has her own jail cell with her own bed and toilet and stuff?" Chase asks.

"Why do you care?" asks Sam. "She's a criminal."

"Yes, that's what it means, Chase," says Mom, ignoring Sam's comment.

It's the beginning of a long and painful process of prosecuting Waldy. It will take another year to reach an initial sentence, and two more before we'll have a final conclusion on my case, which now has a name: The State of Florida vs. Waldina Flores. A new cast of characters enters my life straight out of an episode of *Law & Order: Special Victims Unit*. There's Dennis Siegel, assistant state's attorney and chief sex crimes prosecutor for Broward County. There are Waldy's two lawyers, public defender Ryal Gaudiosi and, eventually, another appointed private attorney, Charles Kaplan, who will both represent Waldy before it's all finished. And then there is a series of judges who hear and rule on each of the grueling, confusing steps in the judicial process.

Dad becomes obsessed with every detail of the case, making it his business to help put Waldy away for as long as possible. I have never seen him so focused, and he's obsessive anyway when it comes to his work. Once, when Dad became particularly frustrated at statements made by Waldy in a hearing, he got into a verbal sparring match with her, leading a bailiff to restrain him. From that point on, Dad was required to sit on the other side of the courtroom, as far away from Waldy as possible. Although I cooperate in everything I'm asked to do, at the start I have ambivalent feelings about prosecuting Waldy. I still wish it could have ended some other way. By the time it's all over, in 2004, I will have gotten to a different place.

That's when I understand the importance of keeping pedophiles like Waldy from ever having the chance to harm another child. Just look at what Waldy was doing when she was caught in Oklahoma: coaching ten-year-old girls in soccer. I have no doubt that she was already sizing up those girls to select her most vulnerable prey, the neediest and loneliest, and thus most open to her advances.

The sad reality is that even if it's your mother or a mother figure, it's not enough to get predators away from their victims; they should be prosecuted for their crimes. If guilty, they have to be jailed and if and when they're released, the state has to monitor them for the rest of their lives. The really bad news is that very few, if any, child sexual abusers are rehabilitated sufficiently to stop preying on children, even after serving long jail sentences.

The Broward County Circuit Court finds that probable cause does exist for having issued the arrest warrant charging Waldy with five felonies. Those charges against her include four counts of sexual battery in a familial custodial setting where the victim is between the ages of twelve and seventeen years, and one count of lewd and lascivious molestation of a minor.

Back then, I didn't have a clue what the word "lascivious" meant. When I looked it up in the dictionary, I found this:

> *Lascivious: adjective. 1. inclined to lustfulness; wanton; lewd: a lascivious, girl-chasing old man.*[1]

Oh, I thought, *so just exchange the word "woman" for "old man" —or anyone whose major preoccupation in life is their own lust, who has a sense of entitlement that they should be able to get their huge sexual needs met no matter what the cost to anyone else.*

At first I don't understand how they come up with "five specific charges" when Waldy had abused me hundreds of times. Dad

---

[1] *Dictionary.com, based on the Random House Dictionary, http://dictionary.reference.com/browse/lascivious.*

explains that each count represents one incident of sexual abuse. These five counts, I learn, aren't supposed to cover all the sexual or physical abuse that happened in the five years Waldy spent with us. Rather, they represent the sum total of abusive acts she committed against me. The fact that these five incidents occurred in the single year preceding the one we're in will theoretically make them easier to prove in court. If Waldy is convicted on all five counts, she can be sentenced to life in prison. In December of 2001, she pleads not guilty to the charges. And so the stage is set for our legal battle.

January, 2002

As you know from earlier chapters, Waldy's arrest brings a horde of press to our doorstep who report every phase of the legal process. I am no longer an anonymous victim. And even though Waldy is behind bars in Fort Lauderdale with no bail, I'm still feeling very paranoid. I wake up at night terrified that she'll escape and come after me. I'm such a wreck that I stay home from school from the day she's brought back to Florida and the charges are made public all through the holidays.

By January of 2002, I'm feeling slightly better, so I agree with my parents that it's time to go back to school. When I return, my teachers and most of my fellow students are supportive, meaning they treat me the same as before. Only a few nasty kids call me a "pervert" or a "dyke." One girl I had liked calls me on the phone to insist that I explain to everyone we know in common that our friendship was "not like that." Other kids are curious and can't keep themselves from asking things like, "So how did she rape you anyway?" I can't really blame them for being confused. It's not like this is something any of them have ever heard of before. Through all of it, I'm fortunate to have Kris's loyalty and affection, and that of my family who likewise never wavers in their support.

Something unexpected that happens is typified by a conversation I have at school with a girl I'll call Rene. She's my age, but shorter than me and petite. I don't know her very well because she's so quiet and shy. One afternoon, I'm standing in the hallway with Kris between classes when Rene approaches me and says, "Can I talk to you?" Then, with a glance at Kris, she adds, "Alone." Kris walks away with a resigned look, saying, "I'll meet you at lunch."

"What's the matter?" I ask Rene.

She's trembling, her mouth and jaw held so tight I wonder if she'll even be able to talk. She looks both ways before she begins.

"Would you believe me if I told you my father raped me?"

"Oh, Rene," I say. "Of course I believe you. Does your mother know?"

"No, I'm too afraid to tell her."

"Yeah. Telling is hard. But I don't know what else you can do. Has it happened more than once?"

She nods, as tears fall onto her cheeks.

I put my hand on her forearm and squeeze it. I don't know what else to do.

"I gotta go," she says as she walks away.

When I see Rene in the hall after that conversation, she always averts her eyes. Then I notice that she leaves school in the middle of the semester. It's from incidents like this that I begin to understand the scope of the problem of child sexual abuse. It knows no gender, class or ethnic boundaries.

My ability to go back to school and pick up my life I credit to the counseling I'm getting from Mandy at the Broward County Sexual Assault Treatment Center. As Mandy explains to me, there are distinct stages you have to go through to recover from sustained sexual abuse. The process takes place in a particular order, and it takes however long you need it to take—years for most survivors. Only the individual can say how long she (or he) needs. This is especially hard for loved ones to understand. With the best of intentions, they give you the message that you should "hurry up and get over it." Sorry, it doesn't work like that. (I share more specifics about my healing process in Appendix A: Facts and Fictions about Child Abuse at the back of this book. I encourage you to check it out, especially if you are also a victim of abuse, as I imagine many of you are.)

After I am treated for my anorexia, I begin the really hard work of allowing my memories of abuse to return in therapy sessions with Mandy. Even at this stage, when I'm just seventeen, it is hard to remember some incidents that happened when I was thirteen and fourteen. I have the most difficulty confronting those times when I went to Waldy for a hug or a few words of reassurance, but she turned it into sex. I feel guilty for having needed her, and I have a deep sense of shame about going along with the sex without protesting louder or telling someone sooner. Of course, that's how your abuser keeps you quiet over the long haul: by reinforcing the mistaken impression that because you didn't prevent it, you deserve what he or she gave you.

March, 2002

Beginning in this contentious year and a half, Dad learns a

surprising lesson about how badly the judicial system treats victims of abuse. In fact, he sees how it can make things so much worse for us. Being who he is, when obstacles come up for me in the legal process, he decides to fight not just for me, but to get laws changed or new ones made that will help others in my position.

That's what happens after my "victim advocate" (someone appointed by the court to help each victim of a crime through the judicial process) suggests that I get an HIV test to make sure Waldy hasn't infected me during our sexual contact. When Dad hears this in January of 2002, he immediately goes to the state's attorney's office and asks how we can do this. Dennis Siegel discovers that granting a victim's request for an HIV test of the accused is not automatic. We find it almost impossible to believe that others haven't insisted on it before us. Siegel then seeks permission of the court by filing a motion to require that Waldy have an HIV test and share the result with us. Unfortunately, the judge sits on our request for three months. It isn't until the end of March that the order for Waldy to take an HIV test is issued. Even then, the judge says she may or may not reveal the outcome of the test because of the defendant's right to privacy.

"What about my rights?" I ask Dad when he shares these developments, or the lack of them. "Don't I get to know if I might have AIDS?"

It's the first of many times that Dad explains to me that there are lots of laws on the books and rights embedded in the state and federal constitutions to protect criminal defendants. He says that the original purpose of these laws was to make sure everyone in America got a fair trial, and that this is what makes our democracy great. But the pendulum has clearly swung too far in that direction if we can't, after three months, get the outcome of an HIV test when

I *may be at risk for infection and not know it.* Because it can take many months to develop the virus after an exposure, only by testing Waldy will I know for sure if I'm in danger.

Dad is so frustrated that he decides we have to take action. Even though the state legislative session is almost over, Dad persuades some legislators to introduce a bill to change the status quo where HIV testing is left to a judge's discretion, and make it automatic. He even brings me along with him to Tallahassee to talk to legislators and explain why a new HIV testing law with mandatory full disclosure to victims is needed. Before we go to our first meeting, Dad explains that it's important to "put a face" on a crime so that legislators understand who will be served by a proposed law. And since many of them have known me since I was "Little Lauren," tagging along with Dad through the corridors of the capitol building, my face is apparently very convincing.

The result is that I get Waldy's test results (thankfully, negative) and Florida gets a new statute to guarantee that victims of sex crimes have the automatic right to seek an HIV test from the accused (not necessarily convicted) person and be given the results within forty-eight hours. It's my initiation into the art of advocacy, and the first of many bills and appropriations for sexual assault victims that Dad and I help make happen.

October, 2002

There's another legal battle going on during these same months. Remember Waldy's tape recordings of arguments and other conversations that went on in our house? It turns out that on the day I revealed my abuse and Dad took Waldy home to pack, he waited in the hallway outside her room, not watching what she put in her suitcase. According to Waldy's later testimony in a deposition, she took those tapes with her for protection. Well, whatever she thought or hoped, the tapes backfired on her.

You see, it's illegal under Florida law to audiotape someone on the phone or in person without the individual's permission. So Waldy doing that would have only added another set of charges to the five counts she was already facing. Ultimately, these charges weren't added, but legal motions and hearings about the tapes caused a six-month delay in Waldy's prosecution. Apparently, Waldy's friend Carla mailed the tapes, which Waldy had taken with her to Oklahoma, to the public defender's office after her arrest. But instead of turning the tapes over to the state's attorney as possible evidence in the case (after determining they would hurt, not help Waldy's defense), the public defender mailed them back to Carla.

Dad files a protest with the Florida state bar alleging the public defender's conduct to have been unethical, prompting the public defender's office to be recused from the case. And that's how Waldy gets private attorney Charles Kaplan appointed to defend her, at the taxpayer's expense. Although the tapes were ultimately never entered as evidence, remarks Waldy made in depositions about them provide a view of how she intended to use them to defend herself against the sexual abuse charges in a trial.

In answers Waldy gives to questions from Assistant State's Attorney Dennis Siegel, she explains that while still living and working in our home, she kept a tape recorder under her pillow at all times (if she did, I never saw it). She goes on to say in her deposition that late on the night before the day she was ordered to leave our house, I came in and told her that she would be sorry for the rest of her life because of what she had said the day before to Kris (this late-night conversation never happened).

Waldy also makes false claims about things Dad supposedly said on that final day. For example, she says that in the car Dad said he knew the accusations against her weren't true and that they had been instigated by Kris out of jealousy. Finally, in the deposition Waldy claims that she taped a conversation where she said the following to me: "Please leave me alone, you need to back up a little bit and look for a boyfriend or something. Just leave me alone because I'm just your nanny."

Of course, as the previous pages explain in more detail than I would ever have wished to share, she never said this or anything like it to me. She was the perpetrator, not me. Waldy testifies in her deposition that she asked Carla to burn the tapes after they were returned to her by the public defender. Still, as I said, their purported relevance to the case provided grounds for months of legal maneuvering and delays.

Starting in January of 2002, we have to begin the difficult process of deciding whether to bring our case to a public trial. At a trial, I would have to testify in front of a jury about all the details of my abuse. I would then be cross-examined; something I'd been warned would be grueling, as I'd be pressed to discuss details of each of the awful, perverted acts that occurred. This would then be written about in newspapers and shown on TV for families to see over dinner. We would then have to take our chances with a jury. Of course, if the state's attorney offered Waldy a plea, she would have to consider it, and she could say no. This is exactly what happens when we discuss a plea with the state's attorney and he then makes the formal offer of a ten-year sentence.

Waldy, through her attorney Charles Kaplan, sends back her response to our offer in a note: "Please tell Mr. Book to go fuck himself."

"Okay," we say to Siegel, "we're going to trial."

Easier said than done. Before a trial can even be scheduled, another half-dozen more motions are filed, each requiring a hearing before a judge, with each court session attended by Dad, and often Mom and me, too. Finally, the trial is set for October 11, 2002, which bizarrely is the day before I turn eighteen. *Wow, just how I want to spend my eighteenth birthday,* I think dejectedly when I hear the news. During all these months in between January and October, I'm dreading what is ahead and trying to prepare myself to testify in front of a jury about all the things I've shared in this book. I can't imagine anything worse, but I feel that I truly have no choice but to go through with it.

Finally, October 11 arrives. But with hours to go before jury selection is to begin, we're told there's another note coming to us from Waldy's defense lawyer. I suppose by this point she's had her own doubts about how she might fare in a jury trial that could result in a sentence of life in prison, because the note says she wants to accept the ten-year plea deal. However, Dad and I, having resigned ourselves to a trial, are angry enough to ask the state's attorney to counter Waldy's request. Mr. Siegel sends his own note back to the defense team: "On behalf of Mr. Book, no deal and please tell Ms. Flores to go fuck herself."

The offer is a sentence of fifteen years, which Waldy accepts.

The plea agreement allows Waldy to plead "no contest," meaning she doesn't technically admit guilt, but she will apologize in open court for her actions against me and my family.

Finally, we arrive at the courthouse for Waldy's sentencing hearing. Waiting in the hallway for our turn to address the judge, Dad notices I'm shaking, so he puts his arm around me. On the other side of the closed courtroom doors, Dad explains, Judge Ilona

Holmes is reviewing the terms of the plea with Waldy, making sure she's been properly advised of her rights and knows the terms she's agreeing to: fifteen years in prison and another ten years on probation as a sexual offender.

While on probation, Waldy will receive mandatory sex offender treatment; she'll have to live with certain restrictions, such as never being with a person under the age of eighteen without supervision, not living within a thousand feet of a school or day-care facility and not going to places such as parks where minors frequently congregate. I'm satisfied that we're doing everything we can to make sure she'll never be able to harm another child.

It's totally quiet when we walk into the courtroom; I'm already a nervous wreck as Dad and I head to the front while Mom, Sam and Chase take their seats in the gallery.

But what I'm really not prepared for are my feelings when I actually see Waldy sitting in the jury section of the courtroom where she's shackled to several other inmates. She's half the weight she was when I last saw her, looking thin and drawn, so unlike herself a year ago. I can't help but make eye contact with her as I walk in, but then I force myself to look away as I walk down the center aisle to the lectern set up for Dad and me to address the court.

"Good morning," says Judge Holmes.

"Good morning," I respond, my voice hardly above a whisper.

"Don't be nervous," says the judge. "Take a deep breath."

And so I do, before I begin reading the letter I've struggled over for days:

"In the past when I was being cared for, I would think of feeling safe, protected and loved. However, in reality, I felt unsafe and sometimes unloved. I am sad and sorry about the way things have happened and

*turned out. I wish things could have been different.
I really don't wish her any harm at all. I forgive her
for her weaknesses that caused her to hurt me. Things
happened that were wrong and that should never
have happened, especially to a child. The amount of
hurt and loss that I feel is beyond measure."*

And then I read a poem by Elisa Farm that I think expresses it better than any words I could come up with myself:

*"The things I feel will never be over.
It will never be through.
This scar in my life was inflicted
by none other than you."*

I put down my speech and look at the judge, who says simply, "Thank you."

I remember working for many hours on this little speech I gave in court. It's called a "victim's statement" because the person who is hurt gets to describe the consequences they've suffered because of the crime committed against them. Looking back with the perspective I have today, my statement was pretty timid. It reflected just how scared and confused I still was a year after my abuse ended. If I had the opportunity to address my abuser and the court today I would say something quite different. I would look Waldy right in the eyes and say this:

*The things you did to me starting when I was thirteen,
the sex you forced me to have, the beatings you gave
me, and the way you controlled every part of my life
until I got free—these were all evil acts. You exploited
the needs of a broken little girl and continued to
break her in order to gratify your own needs. You stole
my childhood and you killed off the person I might*

have become. You separated me from my parents and sister, and you nearly destroyed our family. But the cruelest thing you did was to brainwash me into thinking that this was love. After years of doing the hard work of healing, I finally understand that you never loved or cared about me. I want you to know that I have forgiven you, but I have not and will never forget the evil things you did to me. I believe the price you must pay for your actions is a fair one. And I thank the court for seeing our case through to this just conclusion.

After I give the victim's statement, it's Dad's turn to speak on behalf of our family. Here's some of Dad's statement from the court transcript.

"That's not to say Ms. Flores didn't do a number of good things while working for us, but to allow that conduct while in our trust, to have done what she did while we trusted her with the care of all three of our children, to sexually assault my daughter, to have beat my daughter, is beyond my ability to comprehend or understand. The pain that we have suffered over the past year is beyond what a parent should ever endure or a family should ever endure."

Everyone's eyes are fixed on Dad while he continues his statement. Up until now, I have successfully resisted looking at Waldy, but just at this point I succumb and involuntarily turn my head to where she's now sitting at the defendant's table, parallel to where we're standing. To my astonishment, Waldy is staring right back at me. When she catches my eye, she begins mouthing a silent message obviously intended for me alone: *"It's okay,"* she says. *"I forgive you. I love you. Everything will work out all right."*

I freeze, unable to stop staring at her. She locks her gaze onto mine with a grave, eerily calm expression on her face that I imagine is meant to underscore her words of "forgiveness" and "love." I'm a sitting target; my resolve to be strong and above guilt over "putting Mom away" is utterly undone by her in a matter of seconds.

At that point, my sister, Sam, notices this nonverbal interaction going on between Waldy and me. She gets out of her seat in the gallery to stand at my side, blocking my view of Waldy. Although I was annoyed with her at the time, looking back I see that once again Sam was trying her best to come to her older sister's rescue. Given no choice, I turn away from Waldy and don't look back for the remainder of Dad's remarks.

> *"The days that my daughter cries, the days that she hurts, the days that she feels depressed are countless and they are endless. We're talking about a child who at one point weighed 114 pounds and then weighed 84 pounds before we knew it. That's pain, your Honor. That's pain trying to find herself from the actions of an individual who did not care. Who did not care what impact she was going to have on this child or the others around her. That, your Honor, is what's wrong and that conduct is reprehensible and that conduct, unfortunately for Ms. Flores, must be punished and must be punished severely."*

The next order of business is Waldy's apology, which is a long, pretty incoherent ramble about how she never meant to hurt me, since she loves me so much, but that she's sorry to have hurt me. Then it seems to me that she contradicts herself when she says, "The only thing I'm guilty of is loving this family." Still, Waldy's statement satisfies the court's definition of an apology, and there's nothing left to do but for Judge Holmes to read through all the counts for which she is to serve fifteen years in the state prison.

Then the judge goes on to read the terms of Waldy's probation, which she explains are in effect during and after her sentence. The restriction that registers most for me is the one that says Waldy is to have "absolutely no contact at all with Lauren Book, Ron Book or the rest of the Book family." No phone calls, no letters, nothing. If she breaks this rule, or any other of the terms of her sentence, she could be given life in prison.

"Do you understand each and every one of these terms of your sentence?" the judge asks Waldy.

"Yes, your Honor," she says.

Legally, my case is settled. It can't be appealed. Despite my setback at seeing Waldy and getting emotionally hooked back into her, I go through with a decision I'd made that morning to speak in my own name, not as "Ron Book's eldest daughter," to the press waiting outside the courtroom. In my statement I say, "Even though my abuser Waldina Flores robbed me of my childhood, tomorrow is my eighteenth birthday, and I vow not to let her rob me of my adulthood." The newspaper headlines read: **VICTIM LAUREN BOOK WITNESS AS FORMER NANNY SENT TO PRISON** and **BOOK'S NANNY APOLOGIZES IN COURT, BEGINS 15 YEAR TERM**.

Despite my brave words, my recovery is nowhere near complete. In fact, the emotional progress I've made over the previous year has just been almost entirely reversed.

9

The Meaning of Love

October 11, 2002

The judge had read aloud for us all to hear the prohibition in Waldy's sentence against writing or calling me. So that day in court should have been the last I saw or heard from her. But it wasn't, because I couldn't let go of my huge sense of guilt about *sending her to prison,* much of this guilt aggravated by the words she mouthed to me during her sentencing. My biggest concern after the hearing was how I was going to let her know how sorry I felt about sending her to prison. This dilemma kept me up till dawn the next day. So what do I do? I take out my little box of stationery engraved with spring flowers and *Lauren Frances Book* on the cover and I write *her* a letter of apology.

> *Dear Waldy,*
>
> *Tomorrow is my B-day. I just want to tell you that I'm sooooo sorry. I want to make sure you're ok. I know you can't write but I pray you are happy and ok. I miss you around the house. Lots has been going*

on. We got a new dog so Oscar has a sister. Her name is Coco. She is so little you would call her a rat. Oh, I'm not sure where I'm going to college but I think somewhere in Orlando. I will always pray for you. I wish we could talk, but I know we can't. So I know from what you said to me in court that you are and will be ok. So why don't you put on some weight Skinnie Minnie. I hope you are not mad at me. I really do. Please do not hate me. I just wanted to let you know I love you & miss you.

Love Lauren

P.S. I put in my lunch $ for the week in case you need anything.

Yes, it's pathetic. I cringe when I read it again. But I'm putting aside my embarrassment to give you some insight into the lasting damage done to an abused kid who has to then report his or her abuser and live with the results of that action. Remember, you can love the abuser but hate what that person did to you. You have the right to make the abuser stop it. If the only way to do that is by reporting the abuse and putting your abuser in jail, and usually it is the only way, that is what you should do. But if you don't stop the abuser for yourself, do it for the next kid who might be hurt. Because there *will* be a next kid. In fact, the statistics say that a pedophile typically commits an average of 123 acts against children before being caught and stopped. Sadly, though it's crystal clear to me now, I really didn't *know* these things back then.

When my apology letter reaches Waldy, she ignores the terms of her probation and puts herself at great risk by writing back. Said another way, she tries to reassert her control over me and milk me for all she can get, but this takes me at least two more years to understand. In the meantime, she writes me letters, lots of them. In these letters she uses different names for me, usually the audacious "Mrs. Flores" or her old favorite, "babe." Here are some highlights.

Babe,

I wish I could be with you this Christmas, because it's the second one with out you and it's killing me! I think of you every day and every night. Please think of me this holidays and be happy knowing that we will be together if you want soon.

Dreaming of you always. Teamo, yo.

Hey Baby Happy New Year,

. . . You know what is so funny, the only person who can get me out of here early is you and you don't know what to do. At least you know Jeb Bush who is the person who is making me stay here all this time. He can send me home any time he feels like it. You know he has the power to do that?

I feel sad and hurt that I can't be with the people I love. Why this has to happen baby? Why? Am I a bad person? Do I need to be punish like this? Why? I'm sorry I know you don't have the answers . . .

Thank you for the money, but the tennis shoes are $65 so I'll wait until I get some more money. Thank you *very much baby. Tell me, how is mom and Chase?*

I love you with all my heart.

Always, yo

These letters from Waldy are mailed to me at our house in Plantation. They stop coming after three months, only because Sam intercepts one at the mailbox and gives it to Dad. My poor father doesn't know what to make of this latest bizarre twist in my saga. When he confronts me about the letters, all I can say is that I needed to tell Waldy how sorry I am.

"Why should you be sorry?" he asks, working hard to restrain his anger. "Don't you see she's just abusing you all over again?"

I didn't see it, not yet. I had fallen back to where I was before: Waldy pulling my strings, controlling my thoughts and actions, except that now she was thirty miles away in a state women's prison. Not down the hall from me.

Dad presents Waldy's letters, about a dozen, to Assistant State's Attorney Siegel and asks what can be done to stop her from writing to me. Once again, it's hard to believe that it's not already against the law for a convicted criminal to write to or call their victim. But we find out it's not. Siegel takes a novel approach and asks that Waldy be charged with a violation of her probation, since the judge in her sentencing hearing specifically read the terms of her probation into the record and said that if Waldy violated them, her probation *would be revoked.*

This precipitates another year and a half of legal maneuvering. Due process requires I give another deposition, this time just focused on the letters and not so much on the abuse that came before them, and several more hearings. It generates more newspaper headlines and many more sleepless nights for me. Fortunately, I have help during this next difficult year, as I try to extricate myself from Waldy's psychological hold over me. I bring copies of her letters with me into therapy with Mandy, and together we deal with what they reveal about my deepest feelings. It's really the same work I had been doing before I saw Waldy in court and lost so much ground, only now I'm fixated on Waldy again, not focused on myself as I should be. The crux of the work we are doing is my freeing myself from guilt and shame for daring to think of myself as a separate person with my own identity, rights and needs.

Ironically, the legal storm around the letters probably makes my psychological healing process go faster. It forces me to confront the vestiges of Waldy's brainwashing that make me slip back into delusions about the nature of our five-year relationship, especially the notion that she loved me and cared for me. And my assumption that her sexual torture of me, just like her beating me until I was black and blue and urinating on me, were all part of our "love relationship."

January 15, 2004

Here I am giving that second deposition, this time dealing with the current charge that Waldy "substantially violated her probation" by writing to me. I'm talking again with Waldy's lawyer, Charles Kaplan. With us in the room are Dennis Siegel and my therapist, Mandy Wells. Mandy is given special permission to accompany me because, as we explain to the defense and state's attorney, I'm emotionally distraught about having to face legal questioning about the very thing I'm struggling with in therapy: my inability to psychologically separate from Waldy's control over me. With Mandy there, I'm more likely to get through it without falling apart. Defense attorney Charles Kaplan gets right to the point.

Q. Didn't you expect her to write back?

*A. No. I knew she couldn't. Dennis told me that after the
sentencing hearing when I asked him. There's nothing saying
that you can't write her, but she can't write you. That's all
that was said.*

Q. Is your father mad at you about these letters?

*A. No. He really doesn't understand them, but he's not angry
at me.*

Q. Did you mean the things you said in them?

*A. At the time I did. I look at them now and say, Oh God, at
that time I was lost. More than I am now. And I realize that
that's just not going to happen—running off to Honduras
after she got out of jail.*

This last question and answer refer to later letters in which
I wrote things like *"Promise me we will be together again,"* and
Waldy's response where she says, *"Yes, we'll be together as long as
you're willing to wait for me."* There are also exchanges between the
two of us about how, when she gets out, we'll finally act on her plan
to marry and go off to Honduras where we'll own a coffee ranch.
The questioning by attorney Kaplan on this part of the letters gets
pretty tough.

*Q. You write "promise me we will be together again" and you
don't think she'll write back?*

A. I didn't think she would.

*Q. Well, you're talking about missing how "her skin feels."
These are warm letters. Would you classify them as love
letters?*

A. They were letters.

Q. Love letters?

A. *I missed her.*

Q. *"If you hold me in your arms I could die happy knowing that you would hold and keep my soul. I would live forever." I mean this is very nice. You never thought she'd write back?*

A. *No.*

Then Siegel interrupts, saying, "I know there are a lot of letters and I think she's already expressed why she wrote those things in the letters. You can ask it a hundred times and get the same answer a hundred times."

Of course there are psychological complexities that are hard for many people to understand about why an abused person seeks out her abuser so doggedly, the way I did here. But Kaplan has other reasons for probing into my psyche in this deposition; he's trying to build an argument to take to the probation hearing that says it's my fault for enticing Waldy into writing these letters to me, once again blaming the victim. And victimizing me a second—no, third or fourth time. Back to Kaplan.

Q. *Did you think the things Waldy wrote in her letters to you were mean?*

A. *After a while, after sitting on the letters . . . I kind of said to myself there's something more going on here than just "I'm okay here." I think now even more strongly that those letters were solely written to get me to do things for her.*

Q. *Like what?*

A. *Money. To talk to the governor for instance, to get her out.*

Before this point, I had not yet been able to see Waldy's letters as a reflection of her pathological need to control me in every way she still could: by asking for money, by urging me to use my father's political clout to contact Governor Bush and ask for her release and by insisting on the possibility of a future life we could still have together living on a ranch in Honduras.

How I respond to something that happens toward the end of the deposition reveals a big psychological turning point for me. It captures my surprise and hurt reaction when I find out that Waldy has handed over all my letters, the ones I sent to her in prison, along with a list of things I sent her, like my report card, photos from Christmas and receipts from several money orders I'd enclosed with letters. But my stomach does a flip when he holds up one last thing I sent her: an unsigned card with just the name of a song written on it. The song "Kiss the Rain" is one Waldy and I used to listen and sing along to all the time. I am crushed to see this card in Mr. Kaplan's hands at the deposition.

> Q. So you send this when she's already back here in court for the violation?

> A. I can explain this. She had turned in my other letters and I needed to decide if this was going to be over for me. Meaning was I still going to care, was I still going to be this nice little girl, was I still going to look over in court and fall apart? I said to myself, Okay, I'm going to test her. I'm going to write one more letter and I'm not going to sign it . . . And if she turned it over to you, I knew she didn't care. She didn't care if I got in trouble.

> Q. So it's a really bad thing that I'm showing you this letter then, huh?

> A. Well, no, it's a good thing because I realize she doesn't give a damn about what happens to me. She never did give a damn how what she did was going to hurt me. She never cared at all.

> Q. How would you get in trouble?

A. *Not from the court or anything like that, but I promised Mandy, I promised my parents, I promised myself that I was never, ever going to fall into this trap again. I wanted to get better at this point. And if you read the letters, they're not from a very well person obviously. I wanted to be better.*

Q. *But she's looking at pretty much the rest of her life in prison. You don't think that she should give this [my last card] to me?*

A. *If she truly believed anything that she wrote in her letters, or if she believed in all the lies she told me, during those five years that she was in my house, no. Because then she never really cared for me in the first place. All she was doing was using me for something she wanted.*

Q. *You're pretty angry right now?*

A. *No, I'm not angry . . . this has just proven everything. It was probably the best thing I could have done for myself. She never cared and I'm glad I know that now.*

Q. *Why do you say that?*

A. *Because if she did, she wouldn't have betrayed me. Probably up until the point she was in jail, I still wasn't very sure about what was going on. I was very confused. Everything was kind of mushed up in my head. Was what was going on a real thing or a fake thing? It was all very gray . . . But now it's very clear.*

As cockeyed as my reasoning process may have been to get to this realization that Waldy never truly cared about me, that she always put her own interests first, I did finally get there. I came to understand that the relationship was never based on love, but on her opportunistic desire to get sexual gratification along with financial and (perhaps) emotional benefits through her total control of a malleable child. While caring acts took place in our relationship, they were a means to an end. Even her attorney's attempts to sway the judge presiding over her probation hearing weren't convincing about Waldy's motives. The judge rejected his argument that my writing letters to Waldy justified her writing to me. He further rejected Mr. Kaplan's attempt to change the subject by bringing in evidence, namely testimony from our family therapist, Dr. Levin, that Waldy had been the only stable influence in our home.

As far as the judge was concerned, it didn't matter what I was thinking when I wrote to Waldy, or how dysfunctional our family was before and after Waldy got there. Waldy was an adult inmate with very clear rules set for her probation as a sex offender. They prohibited her from contacting me, her victim, ever again. End of story. She was found guilty of probation violation and an additional ten years, the original term of her probation, was added to her sentence, although Dennis Siegel argued for a life term. Under Florida law, Waldy will serve 85 percent of her twenty-five-year sentence. That means she will spend at least twenty-one years in prison.

I went back to trying to extricate myself from the psychological cage Waldy had erected around me, which I had willingly stayed in during those years she was with us. To put it in very non-technical terms, abuse and other forms of trauma get stuck in your body. This blocked energy keeps you from feeling much of anything and from enjoying life. Sometimes the aftereffects of abuse make it impossible to do simple things, like standing in a crowded room, hearing a balloon pop or opening up to someone you don't know, even if it's a therapist who is trained to help you. For me, the abuse got stuck in my stomach; so firmly that I found it difficult to leave the house without wrapping a towel around my waist as if to protect my tummy. Believe me, this was pretty noticeable in Florida, where people wear T-shirts and shorts most of the year. Two therapy techniques helped me get unstuck and reclaim my stomach and, eventually, my peace of mind.

Guided visualization is like meditating, but there's someone (your therapist) talking you through the process of first centering and then exploring scary feelings and memories. Some people find hypnosis valuable for doing this same thing. In my case, because of my abuse, I wasn't able to let go and trust someone enough to let go of control like that. In other words, I wasn't a good candidate for hypnosis. Guided visualization is a gentler way of doing the same work.

Another technique I found to deal with the aftereffects of my sexual abuse is called EMDR, or eye movement desensitization and reprocessing. Through different methods, EMDR helps you get in touch with feelings and painful memories that have been blocked. Once when I did EMDR, I got a vivid memory of the navy blue carpet on Waldy's bedroom floor in our house in Aventura. From that visual fragment, the whole scene came back to me when she slammed my head between the frame of her bed and the wall. That was the first time she physically abused me to the point of bruising, and I had repressed it. Remembering that incident allowed me to excavate the source of my night terrors, and that helped me begin to let go of them.

There was a lot else going on in my life during the two years it took for these legal and psychological struggles to play out. For one thing, I finished high school. Not only finished it—I graduated with a 3.7 GPA, and in my senior year I was elected homecoming queen. It occurred to me at the time that my classmates may have picked me out of pity, or because they felt bad about shunning me right after I came back to school in the midst of all the media coverage about Waldy. But that possibility didn't take away from the fun of being homecoming queen; wearing a crown and marching into the gym with everyone cheering and taking pictures felt like a real healing for me. I was no longer that victim with a sign over her head that read "Damaged Goods." I was a young woman accepted and honored for herself.

I'd come full circle from the anonymous victim I was at the beginning of my junior year to the advocate I became when, in the spring of my senior year, I organized a schoolwide assembly. The topic was child sexual abuse. With kids from first to twelfth grades in the audience, Detective Juanita Reid, Assistant State's Attorney Dennis Siegel, Mandy Wells from the Broward County Sexual Assault Treatment Center, Dad and I presented a panel discussion about what sex abuse is, and how kids can get help if it is happening to them. Right after the panel ended, six students sought out Detective Reid and Dennis Siegel and asked for their cards, so they could call and talk privately about something or someone troubling that came up as a result of the presentation.

September, 2003

Another whole chapter of my life begins when I leave Miami to go to a small private college in Orlando. There I live alone in an apartment off campus. It's the first time I've ever been on my own, away from my family. Kris and I are still dating, and he comes up from Miami to visit me every other weekend. But the rest of the time in Orlando, I'm alone. While I'm there, I discover some new things about myself. For one thing, I find it's very hard for me to make new friends. I simply don't trust people like I used to. There's also a delayed reaction to the abuse that shows up in how I dress. Even though it's warm for most of the year in Orlando, I pretty much always wear several layers of clothing: a T-shirt, a long-sleeved sweatshirt, sometimes a bulky sweater or coat on top. I get some strange looks, but no one says anything; no one knows me well enough to try and get through my armor.

An academic counselor I see from time to time is the first person who finally asks me why I overdress like this. Oddly, I'm not really aware of it until she says something. When I get in touch with my therapist back in Miami to ask her about it, she explains that this behavior is typical for sexual abuse victims. We do it to cover up our bodies because of a desire for protection and out of a lingering sense of shame over what's been done to us.

With a few bumps in the road, I make it through freshman year really well, even after I have to return in January to give my deposition on Waldy's letters. During the spring semester of that year, I sometimes join Dad up in Tallahassee to help lobby for another new law that grows out of my case. It comes about after Dad sees how getting the letters from Waldy hurt my recovery. Passed in the 2004 legislative session, this law unequivocally requires Florida's courts to prohibit people convicted of sexual battery, following their convictions, from contacting their victims, making any violation a severe third-degree penalty offense. They name it *The Lauren Book Protection Act*, and it's signed into law by Governor Jeb Bush in May. There's a picture on Dad's office wall of the signing ceremony, with me, this still skinny, awestruck girl standing next to the governor. Looking at it, I think how it's a far cry from asking the governor to let Waldy out of prison. Thank goodness.

After my freshman year, I have enough credits and the grades I need to transfer to the University of Miami and move into my own place near campus. Finally, the legal proceedings and all personal contacts between Waldy and me are done for good. Or so I thought.

About five years ago, Waldy managed to terrorize my family one last time. According to a cell mate of hers who communicated with Dad from prison by mail and telephone, Waldy attempted to have two departing inmates kidnap Chase and me, in retribution for what I'd done to her. This threat, although it may sound fantastic and impossible, was subsequently investigated by the Office of the State Attorney and the Florida Department of Law Enforcement, who found it credible enough to post armed deputies at my parents' home (where Chase still lived). When I went to the house in Plantation to see for myself, I could hardly believe the weird scene: an officer with a shotgun stationed at the front and back doors, and mug shots of these two parolees posted throughout the neighborhood.

After ten days of this round-the-clock protection, the sheriff advised Dad to take the family and leave the area until the ex-inmates could be apprehended. That's when Mom, Dad, Sam, Chase and I took an unplanned ten-day cruise. While we were away, the two ex-inmates were caught, charged with violating parole and sent back to prison. Waldy was moved into seclusion and then sent to another, higher-security facility in the state, where she remains today, serving her sentence and leaving me free to live my life without fear of her physical presence.

In my sophomore year at the University of Miami, I am nineteen years old, and my personal relationship with Kris, who's also attending UM, continues to be strong. We begin to talk about getting married after we graduate. I'm studying elementary education and creative writing. I already know that among the things I am going to do is work on behalf of victims of sexual abuse, and for the prevention of abuse against kids. What form that work might take I won't know for a few more years.

10

Walk in My Shoes

I graduate from the University of Miami in 2008 with a BSE, cum laude, in elementary education. There are other important endings and beginnings that year. I marry Kris Lim, the boy I started dating in the ninth grade, who helped me gather the courage to report my abuse and who stuck by me during the tough years of recovery that followed. He's the only boyfriend I ever had, and I thought we would be together for life. I wish I could say our marriage has a fairy-tale ending of happily ever after, but unfortunately that's not the case.

Kris becomes a professional golfer after graduating from UM, a career that separates us a great deal of the time. But we manage to keep our marriage thriving, until I discover a betrayal that nearly devastates me. Kris has an affair with the roommate of one of my closest girlfriends. We make an attempt at marriage counseling, but Kris opts out before we can repair the broken trust he's created. Infidelity is hard on any marriage. But as an abuse survivor, it's especially difficult for me to experience another betrayal and loss of trust in someone I've cared so much about for so long.

I have moved on since the breakup of my marriage and I'm going on the only way I know how, one step at a time. Once again, I'm blessed to have the support of family and close friends, who I thank from the bottom of my heart. I'm also thankful for the work I'm committed to, which keeps me going every day.

Right after graduation, I spend a year teaching kindergarten in the Miami-Dade public schools. I love working with kids that age, but I keep feeling like I have a bigger job to do. That's when I move into full-time advocacy for abused kids through the foundation I've created, *Lauren's Kids*. In 2007, the foundation becomes a nonprofit corporation and we begin operating out of our office in Aventura. Over the last few years, we've operated a twenty-four-hour crisis hotline, worked on and successfully passed a dozen new laws, raised ongoing funds for sexual assault treatment centers in Florida and created a kindergarten to fifth-grade curriculum to teach kids how to protect themselves from sexual predators who may already be in their intimate circle.

As I close, I want to share with you one of Lauren's Kids biggest triumphs: our first Walk in My Shoes Survival Walk to raise awareness and support legislation to protect children from sexual assault. I decide to do it in April, because that's National Sexual Assault Awareness Month. When I first propose the idea of this 500-mile walk in 2009, my Dad thinks I'm truly crazy.

"Do you have any idea how tough it is to walk 500 miles?" Dad asks me.

"No, not really. But I'm sure I can get in shape for it," I answer.

Well, at first I really don't know what I'm talking about. But once I make up my mind, Dad can tell I'm not going to be deterred. After talking to trainers who help people get ready for marathons, I begin my training, which consists of walking twenty miles a day while wearing a weighted vest, five days a week.

But I find there is plenty to do besides physical training to organize a 500-mile walk; for example, getting permits and putting the word out to media, celebrities and the public to get involved. I make hundreds of phone calls to enlist political leaders and sports figures like Miami Dolphins fullback Lousaka Polite, quarterback Tyler Thigpen and former wide receiver Nat Moore, along with NBA All-Stars Dwyane Wade and Alonzo Mourning, who join us for different legs of the walk. Another important part of our preparations is getting the directors and staff of sexual assault treatment and recovery centers to join us for media appearances at malls, libraries and government offices along the route. This way, we make sure these local heroes get their work better known to people in their own areas. At each stop, we make it a point to bring press to either a rape crisis center or sexual assault treatment center in that city or town. I soon discover that organizing this walk is akin to putting together the logistics for eighteen straight days of public events, and coordinating them with hundreds of people. There are T-shirts and signs to make, vehicles, hotels, food and water to provide, and it goes on and on like this for months.

April 2, 2010

Our Walk in My Shoes Survival Walk starts outside the house in Aventura where my abuse began. With me are Dad, Mom and Chase along with hundreds of volunteers and our celebrity Dolphin players. Dolphins CEO Mike Dee comes and brings the entire Dolphins' cheerleading squad with him. *How very strange to be back here in this way,* I think, as I look around at the wild scene of those walking with us, reporters and neighbors filling the sidewalks and the streets.

When a reporter asks me why I'm standing here making all this fuss in a neighborhood where I don't even live anymore, I say, "I want people of all ages to see that it's okay to tell someone about abuses that happen to them. I want them to see me walking and dealing with my ghosts, and think, 'I can face this.'"

Aventura is the first leg of our eighteen-day walk, which begins on Good Friday, April 2, and ends on April 20 at the State Capitol in Tallahassee. There are twenty of us who are core walkers. On that first day, we walk fifteen miles from Aventura to the Broward County Sexual Assault Treatment Center where I received so much help. Remembering my time there as a victim, I make an emotional speech to the assembled crowd, which includes many other women and girls who are former as well as present clients of the center. Although these women are only supposed to walk one symbolic mile with us after we leave the center, I'm incredibly touched and energized when they stick it out for fifteen miles.

Also there for the start of the walk is an older woman named Penny, who, though she's really not fit enough to walk insists on coming nonetheless, explaining that she had been sexually abused as a younger woman, as had her granddaughter. When Penny falls and we convince her that she needs to get her bleeding knee treated, she gives me a key chain and asks me to carry it with me, so she'll be part of the walk to the end. Penny then shows up several more times at stops along the march to cheer us on and walk a few steps more.

Along the way, we're joined by hundreds of people who pick up signs and walk with us. In Jupiter on April 6, we're walking along the road when an African-American mother brings her young daughter next to me, so she can hear me personally explain the safety facts the mother thinks she needs to know. I don't ask why.

Our route takes us up U.S. 1 on the east coast of Florida, across the center of the state to Orlando and Tampa, through Ocala and Gainsville, over to St. Augustine, up to Jacksonville and across the northern tier counties to Tallahassee. We walk thirty to thirty-five miles a day, two days on and one day off, staying in hotels on our route. Even though I've trained hard to get in shape, it's really hard to keep walking like this. Once you sit or lie down, you don't want to get up. You get blisters and sunburn. But what makes it all worthwhile is the people who come—either because they planned to or because they spontaneously join us—especially the ones who tell me their own stories of abuse. Many of them are telling for the first time.

We walk into Orlando on April 9, arriving at the Kissimmee Sexual Assault Treatment Center at noon. A woman named Kim says she was abused as a child by her stepfather, as were her sister and brother. Kim told her mother at the time, but her mother didn't believe her. On the walk, she says that being part of our group makes her feel alive again. Another young woman pulls me aside at a mall to tell me that she's so depressed about her own abuse that she has felt ending her life is her only option. But after being there and hearing from other survivors, she says, "Okay . . . I'm going to get counseling and try to make it."

I think the last five miles of each day are the hardest, because I feel like I'm carrying all the survivors I've met on my back; they're helping me get there, but also counting on me. In Daytona Beach, with a knee brace on each leg, I'm so exhausted, sore and depleted that I collapse in my hotel room, telling Dad that I don't think I can go any further. He leaves me to rest saying we can decide in the morning. That night I get a call of support from NBA All-Star Dwyane Wade, who tells me that it's normal to feel this way, but urges me to push through the pain and keep going. That's when the purpose of what I'm doing really sinks in: my walking these five hundred miles is the physical manifestation of the emotional and spiritual struggle I've had over these past nine years. This walk needs to be an annual event, so that other survivors can experience the same sense of victory and closure I'm now feeling.

Sometimes it's the nonverbal shows of support that boost my spirits. The police chief in Port St. Lucie who gives me a big hug, the homeless man who insists I take his $5 donation and the kids and adults who wave at us from the side of the road.

In Tampa, we make one of our last stops at the campus of the University of South Florida, where at our Take Back the Night rally I make a special point of speaking about the epidemic of sexual assaults and date rapes on campuses like this one.

April 20, 2010

The last leg of the Walk in My Shoes Survival Walk takes me and several hundred others onto Apalachee Parkway, which is mostly all uphill into the center of Tallahassee, until we reach the Capitol Building. It's so exciting to be this close to the end; and yet I'm so beyond tired and it's so hot, I'm afraid I'll faint before I reach the finish line. The tears start and I can't stop crying as we approach the Capitol. Then when I see that I'm almost there, I get a burst of energy and sprint the last eight hundred yards, collapsing on the capitol steps, amazed and overwhelmed with emotion that we've made it. My fellow walkers catch up to me and let out hoots and hollers to announce our victorious arrival.

These steps are where we hold our final rally of the walk at noon. As I look out into the crowd, I see that nearly everyone is wearing our turquoise Lauren's Kids Foundation T-shirts. In the audience and offering endorsements at the lectern are some seventy state legislators who've come out to cheer us on, including the senate president Jeff Atwater of Palm Beach, who, when he's given the microphone, thanks me, saying, "You've made Florida a better place." He also announces that the Florida State Senate and House have that day taken up resolutions to commend the walk and our cause.

Larcenia Bullard, state senator from Miami, speaks about her own experience of being sexually molested by her father. "I stand as one who has had that experience and I stand for others who have been afraid to speak out. I pray for Lauren that she will really complete her journey because her journey has just begun. By speaking out, she is helping so many others come to a point where they too will feel better about themselves." There are tears on the faces of many in the crowd when Senator Bullard finishes.

Rain clouds are threatening as I get up to give my speech. After thanking everyone for coming, I share a little bit of my story of abuse, closing with this:

"I think that the pain I suffered as a child was awful and should never ever happen to a child. But today, it's not so much about pain; I feel elation, excitement, and a huge sense of relief. I'm proud to be here and so glad that I can speak for other survivors."

I thank the legislators for the legislation they passed in the session that's about to end, such as the bill providing financial support for sexual assault treatment centers and raising awareness by instituting a voluntary $1 donation option when people renew their driver's licenses and vehicle registrations. I urge them to continue to work to pass a proposed bill that would end the statute of limitations on sexual crimes against children, a critically important change in the law that has run into strong resistance from the Catholic Conference. I also urge them to support a new bill to impose a tougher penalty on sex offenders who go to places frequented by children, such playgrounds and parks, and that will also provide child safety zones. I beg for tougher sentencing on cyber crimes.

I ask everyone to spread the word that it's okay to tell; and that we each need to do our part to make sure that those who most need to hear it, get this message. I say that 95 percent of sexual abuse is preventable—if children learn to protect themselves and we adults do our part to ensure their safety.

Toward the end of my speech, Florida governor Charlie Crist walks up the steps and gives me a hug. Next to us, I see my father, tears welling in his eyes. We've both worked so hard to make this moment happen. Governor Crist offers words of support, and then, as dark clouds move into place and rain starts falling in big drops, I return to the lectern. I keep it short: "Thank you, everyone! Remember, it's okay to tell. I told and I survived. You will, too."

11

You Get Up Again

April 26, 2010 [2]

"Lauren, what brings you here today?" Grace, a sturdy woman in her thirties with red frizzy hair, hugs me in the front office of the converted strip mall that is Second Chance Recovery House in Jacksonville, Florida. Her affection feels like an electric charge in my exhausted state.

"I had to get gas and I remembered you were right off 95."

Grace puts her arm on my shoulder and leads me to a worn stuffed chair next to her desk. "Fantastic. My day was already made when I heard your news on the radio. Let me gather the ladies in the group room. I want you to tell everyone, and meet some of our new arrivals."

I love this place. All the women who live at Second Chance have been sexually abused and many also come here after dealing with addiction and prostitution before they've even turned eighteen. But thanks to the tight ship Grace runs, they're going back to school, finding jobs and a getting a new start on their lives. I smile when I see on the wall above Grace's desk an embroidered plaque of one

---

[2] *On April 26, 2010, the Florida State Senate and House unanimously voted to do away with the statute of limitations on sexual crimes against children between the ages of twelve and fifteen. I was thrilled to be there with my father to watch the final vote. The legislation was then immediately signed into law by Governor Charlie Crist. When a reporter from the Miami Herald asked me why the law was needed, I said, "Because there is no statute of limitations to a victim's suffering or their recovery. Generally, the pain lasts forever."*

of my favorite slogans: **YOU GET UP AGAIN BECAUSE THE ALTERNATIVE SUCKS.**

In the group room, forty or so young women are settling onto plastic chairs hastily arranged in semicircular rows. Some, whom I've met on previous visits, come up and give me high-fives and hugs. It's a blast of the warmth I've been sorely missing over the past few weeks going from one legislator's office to the next with my father, trying to secure the votes we need.

Grace puts up a hand to quiet her flock. "For those of you who haven't had the pleasure of meeting Lauren Book, this young lady is a marvel to watch as she charms our state legislators at the same time she's twisting their arms until they authorize the funding we need to keep this center and others like it going. Today Lauren has some great news to tell us. Let's give her a big welcome."

Grace's introduction brings applause and whistles, and I'm already feeling recharged as I stand up.

"Thanks. I can't tell you how happy I am to be here. As Grace said, during this legislative session we had a successful vote on a law people have been trying to have passed for many years. It gets rid of the statute of limitations for sexual assault victims who were under the age of sixteen when their abuse happened. Now victims can get their abusers prosecuted no matter how long it takes for them to find the courage to report them. It was a hard battle. We even had the Vatican fighting against us. Do you know why we finally won? Because survivors like us are no longer staying quiet."

Everyone claps their hands, and some stomp their feet to show their approval.

"Every one of us here has a story of abuse and survival. My abuser, who came into my life as my nanny, made me a prisoner in my parents' home for nearly five years. Many nights, I asked God to free me from her absolute control. If he couldn't, I asked that he take me with him, because I couldn't live with it any longer. But after a while I stopped asking."

I see winces of recognition and tears on the faces of some of my listeners. It's a sure-fire way to tell if someone you're talking to is an abuse victim. Dad told me it happens to him, too, when he's talking with men and women in business suits at places like the chamber of commerce. He'll be explaining our issue when suddenly someone starts tearing up. And very often that person goes on to reveal that he was an altar boy molested by a priest, or that she was on a soccer team and raped by her coach, and that he or she had never talked about it until that moment. So many of them are simply looking for an opportunity to feel empowered by finally telling someone who will understand.

Now I gather my thoughts and keep going. "I finally told about my abuse when I was almost seventeen. Although having the truth come out was really painful for me and my family, I was lucky, because they believed me and I got help. As many of you know personally, recovering from sexual abuse is a lot like being a returning solider. We may be out of the line of fire, but in our minds and bodies, the war is still going on."

"Amen," says a young woman in the front row. Murmurs of agreement follow from some others. When it's quiet again, a dark-skinned teenager in the back stands and raises her hand. "Can I ask a question?"

"Sure," I say.

"Don't get me wrong. I believe every word you're saying. But I guess, maybe because your family has money and you're so well spoken and . . ."

"Blond and white," I add, helping her out.

"Uh-huh, that too," the girl says while a ripple of nervous laughter fills the room. "You had so much going for you, how come you let it go on for that long?"

The only sound is the roar of traffic on the interstate as I take a swallow. I want to tell the truest reason I can come up with to this group of women, most of whom have not had any of the advantages I've grown up with.

"I knew something was wrong as soon as she started touching me where no one ever did. But I was a confused, lonely kid and I didn't understand where it was headed until much later. By then I was ashamed, and afraid that my parents might send me away if they knew what had been going on in their house."

The girl who asked the question sits down, and heads are nodding. I'm thinking maybe I should recite the statistics I try to include in my talks, so victims will know they're not alone and other people will get how big the problem really is. The numbers are staggering: one out of three girls and one out of five boys are sexually abused before the age of eighteen, with 90 percent of the abuse perpetrated by someone they love and trust. But I hold off right now, because I'm digging for a deeper answer.

"The reality is I'm still working on that question. I'm twenty-six now and it may take me a while longer to truly understand how my abuser changed me from a regular twelve-year-old kid into a frightened victim who couldn't tell the people who loved her that she desperately needed their help.

"My counselor, Mandy Wells at the Broward County Sexual Assault Center, who helped me during the awful time right after I told about my abuse, said something to me that I've never forgotten. Whenever I would cry and ask when I was going to feel normal again, she'd tell me if I was going to make it, I had to look at healing as a process, not as a destination. The good news is that the process gets easier the more you work at it. That doesn't mean recovery always goes in a straight line; as you all know, there are plenty of twists and turns in that road." I pause to allow some laughs of recognition. "But eventually, yes, I have been able to love and trust people again—most importantly myself. I've learned that I'm the only one who can rescue that little girl who spent too many nights cowering in fear in her bedroom."

"You got that right," a woman off to the side calls out.

"Thank you," I respond. Then I close my eyes and take a deep breath, letting the tension of the week drain out of me, and allowing the support of the women in the room to fill me up. When I open my eyes, I make eye contact with a Latina in the front row whose tears are giving her face a bright sheen, as they reflect rays from the harsh fluorescent lamps on the ceiling. By the way she's holding her arms tight against her chest, it's obvious she's holding back sobs. "Hang in there," I say to her. "You will feel better."

She nods and I return my attention to the whole group. "Someone gave me a line from a song that says it really well: 'There's a crack in everything, to let the light in.' I used to think that I was the only one with a crack. But I've since learned that most people have one. And the light that helps us mend those broken places inside comes from telling and hearing the truth.

"So if we're going to keep all kids safe, we have to make incest and child sexual abuse acceptable topics of conversation. When other people want us to keep quiet because the subject makes them uncomfortable, or when someone questions our memory of events, we have to hold to the truth. Sexual abuse of children is preventable! But we can't wait for someone else to act. We're the ones who have to stop this madness. And it starts with each of us telling our story."

There are more hoots and whistles and applause as I sit down.

My image of the faces in that room, all of them determined and hopeful, keeps me going for days and weeks afterward.

Thank you for reading my story, and for thinking about the tough issues that arise from it. I'm often asked whether I hate Waldy for the acts she committed against me, or if I resent my parents for not being there for me and missing the abuse that went on for all those years. I can truthfully answer no to both questions. Forgiveness is something talked a lot about, but I think not really understood. I know I didn't completely get it until I really started working on myself. What it comes down to is that we're each responsible for our own actions. When I say I work on myself, I mean that I constantly challenge my beliefs and actions, so I can end every day without feeling guilt or shame, and instead experience the joy of being alive and free.

I know that my parents did the best they could with what they knew at the time. I love my mom and dad. I'm also pleased to share with you that my brother and sister are both doing great. Samantha is pursuing fashion design at Savannah College of Art and Design, and Chase studies marine biology at the University of Miami. Our family is stronger and closer today than we would have been if we hadn't experienced this tragedy together.

And even though the acts she committed against me, and who knows how many others, were evil, I don't hate Waldy. When she was young, I believe she probably experienced something close to what she did to me. Where I fault her is in failing to confront her own pain, and then inflicting it on someone else—me. No one should get away with that.

I like to say that I'm the queen of my own shit, just like you're the king or queen of yours. If we don't clean up our shit, it follows us around forever. I'm sorry to use such ugly imagery, but it fits.

Even with the cruelty I faced at Waldy's hands, I feel blessed to have been given all the experiences I've lived through. Everyone faces tragedies or wounds in their lives. I haven't met anyone past the age of eighteen who hasn't. Because I've worked through the pain of my wounds—first the pain of being an emotionally abandoned child and then the trauma created by my abuse—I am the woman I am, the teacher I am and the leader I'm becoming. Because of everything I've experienced, I now have the strength and clarity to speak out on behalf of abused children and other people in need.

So just because you have a wound, it does not mean you're broken or bad. As I said to the women at Second Chance, we're all cracked in some way, but we're also all capable of healing. You are a gift from God, or whatever universal being you may believe in. That means you are connected to me and everyone else God created. No matter how bad your situation is right now, you can get help and your life can be better. The first step is telling. Just remember, *it's always okay to tell*—and when you do, I promise that you will become the hero of your own story.

Facts and Fictions about Child Abuse

What Every Concerned Person Needs to Know

The mistreatment and neglect of children, including physical and sexual abuse, has long been underreported in the United States. This status quo was challenged in 1993 with the enactment of the National Child Protection Act. That law made it a prosecutable offense for anyone coming into contact with children through work or volunteer activities to fail to report any credible suspicions of child abuse. This now includes teachers, doctors, bus drivers, day-care workers, clergy, scout masters and many others.

Although reporting and prosecution increased after this act became law, it should still be assumed that any statistics about child abuse grossly underrepresent the scope of the problem. The causes of this underestimation are complex. In addition to the misplaced shame felt by child victims that inhibits them from telling anyone of their abuse, there is also the threat that they won't be believed, and the possibility that they will be removed from their homes (this occurs in 20 percent of investigated cases) and placed in a fragmented child foster care system. Add to that the frequent negative economic consequences resulting from the jailing of a family's breadwinner and the result is a continued lack of reporting and prosecution of child maltreatment.

THERE ARE FOUR TYPES OF CHILD ABUSE

From the available information, based only on those cases that have been reported, there are four recognized categories of child maltreatment:

NEGLECT

This is the largest category of child maltreatment. Neglect entails a failure to provide for a child's basic physical, educational and psychological needs. It might include child abandonment, failing to provide proper nutrition or medical attention, exposing a child to spousal conflict, and permitting drug and alcohol abuse in the presence of a child.

PHYSICAL ABUSE

Includes beating, slapping, kicking, burning, shaking or otherwise causing physical harm to a child. Studies indicate that most of these cases result from situations of physical punishment in which a parent loses control and punishment escalates into battery.

SEXUAL ABUSE

Includes fondling a child's genitals or breasts, committing intercourse or other sexual acts with a child and exposing the child to indecent acts or involving a child in pornography. As long as a child is induced into sexual activity with someone who is in a position of greater power, whether that power is derived through the perpetrator's age, size, status or relationship, that act is abusive. A child who cannot refuse, or believes she cannot refuse, is a child who has been sexually violated.

PSYCHOLOGICAL ABUSE
Includes verbal put-downs and any other behavior that terrorizes, threatens, rejects, damages or isolates children. There is often overlap between these categories of abuse. For example, psychological abuse nearly always accompanies other forms of abuse and neglect.

VICTIMS OF CHILD ABUSE

A "child" in abuse statistics is anyone age eighteen or under who has been subjected to any of the categories of maltreatment cited above.

How many children are sexually abused?
In one study of sex abuse reports subsequently investigated and verified by authorities, more than half of the child victims reported being subjected to more than fifty incidents of sexual abuse. The average number was 143 incidents. The average age of the first abuse of the children in this study was age seven, although several other studies document the sexual abuse of children starting at under three years of age.

BOYS AS VICTIMS
There is a great deal of misunderstanding about boys as victims of child sexual abuse. Among the most common fictions paired with the facts are these:

Boys are not as traumatized by sexual abuse as girls.
Not so. Studies show boys, most of whom are sexually victimized between the ages of six and ten, are just as traumatized by the

experience as girls. Because of their physiology, boys might experience erection, ejaculation and orgasm. It should be understood that these responses are automatic in males and not indicative of any lessening in trauma from their sexual violation by an adult. The experience of feelings of confusion, guilt, fear, betrayal, shame and anger are gender-neutral in sexual abuse.

Homosexual males perpetrate most sexual abuse of boys.
Wrong. The vast majority of male sexual abusers of boys identify themselves as heterosexual. Another little-known fact: 38 percent of the sexual abusers of boys are female.

Boys abused by males become homosexuals.
Not true. Abuse doesn't determine sexual orientation. It may, however, cause later sexual dysfunction in an adult male, if the individual doesn't receive support and/or treatment for residual emotional problems.

AGES OF VICTIMS
Babies under the age of one have the highest rate of maltreatment. The perpetrators are nearly always their parents. It is thought that babies suffer the most abuse because they have the least ability to regulate their behavior (crying, other forms of distress), thus they're more likely to trigger abusive parental behavior. Sadly, in the United States abuse and neglect are the leading cause of death for children under the age of four.

How many children are physically abused and/or neglected?
The approaches used to make this estimate vary, from 1.2 percent of American children every year to somewhere between 500,000 and 2.5 million on an annual basis who are victims of physical abuse and/or neglect.

Who commits the crime of sexual abuse against children?
In 90 percent of cases of child sex abuse, the perpetrator is someone known to the child: a parent, relative, family friend or other care provider. Only 10 percent of child sexual abuse is perpetrated by strangers.

Who commits physical abuse and neglect of children?
According to state and federal crime statistics, and based only on cases successfully prosecuted, in 72 percent of these cases, the perpetrator is the parent, with mothers representing 56 percent and fathers 16 percent, because, as child abuse experts point out, mothers generally spend more time with children than fathers.

DANGER SIGNS OF CHILD ABUSE

Because child abusers often terrorize their victims into maintaining silence about their abuse, anyone who interacts with children should be aware of potential warning signs that might indicate ongoing abuse.

- Frequent visible bruises or sprained/broken bones
- Sudden emotional withdrawal, depression
- Frequent urinary infections
- Genital bruises
- Sudden aggressive behaviors toward peers
- Trouble sleeping; nightmares
- Displays an irrational fear of certain places, situations or people
- Regression to an earlier stage of development, bed-wetting or thumb sucking
- Acting out in school

- Social isolation
- Frequent school absences
- Inadequate personal hygiene
- Signs of alcoholism or drug addiction in the home

There is one population of children (and adults) that we are becoming increasingly aware faces an extremely high vulnerability to sexual abuse: those with a developmental disability limiting their ability to speak. This includes autistic children as well as other physically and mentally impaired persons. Special attention needs to be given to prevention and monitoring of these populations to prevent their abuse.

Most states require the reporting of any credible evidence of child abuse to law enforcement within forty-eight hours. Any previous privacy pacts between, for example, a minor and his doctor or his psychotherapist become void at such a time. The practitioner is then liable for prosecution if he does not report evidence of such a crime.

EMOTIONAL DISORDERS ASSOCIATED WITH CHILD ABUSE

Psychological research has documented negative effects of abuse on every aspect of a child's life. Some behaviors may begin as defense mechanisms adopted by the child to help him or her survive the abuse. An example is the defensive instinct to split off from one's body or mind while experiencing physical or psychological pain. Another coping mechanism with limited usefulness for many abuse survivors is the repression of painful memories. For many, these behaviors and aftereffects develop into full-blown disorders, or at least negative symptoms that are sustained into the child's adult years.

DEPRESSION

The most common psychological disorder seen in an estimated two thirds of abused children is depression.

POSTTRAUMATIC STRESS DISORDER

Fifty percent of abused children also show signs of posttraumatic stress disorder, or PTSD. This is an anxiety disorder, common to soldiers who've fought in wars and survivors of war and natural disasters. For anyone who has felt intense fear or been threatened with death or injury, PTSD causes flashbacks, nightmares and severe psychological and/or physical symptoms when exposed to stimuli (people, places, sensory experiences) that trigger memories of the trauma. PTSD sufferers are easily startled and often cannot tolerate crowds of people.

PANIC AND OTHER PHOBIAS

Distortions or exaggerations of fear reactions are frequently experienced by child abuse survivors. Agoraphobia, a fear of open spaces, is common. Other fears include fear of driving and a fear of entrapment in small spaces. Such a phobia might make the adult survivor require that a door or window be open at all times.

DISSOCIATION

This occurs when a victim distances their consciousness from the traumatic events. This can manifest later as a "zoning out" from the here and now, or an extreme compartmentalization of emotions. In its extreme form, a person can create multiple personalities to cope with the aftereffects of abuse, known as "dissociative disorder."

BORDERLINE PERSONALITY DISORDER

Mostly associated with child sexual abuse victims, this disorder manifests as a splitting of one's identity and a lack of emotional control. As a result of this splitting, persons with this disorder may be loving and trustful one moment and raging and distrustful moments later—toward the same person. Victims tend to be unable to sustain stable personal, social or professional relationships. They also frequently display self-destructive and impulsive behaviors; for example, driving recklessly and/or engaging in promiscuous sex.

ADDICTION

Addiction to alcohol or drugs frequently serves the need of the survivor of child physical or sexual abuse to numb the pain of his or her memories of abuse. Addiction can be to an activity such as gambling or shopping as much as to a substance. Alcohol dependence also serves to temporarily overcome the social phobia common to abuse victims. Often, an addiction then becomes an additional disorder the adult abuse survivor must face.

EATING DISORDERS

Child sexual abuse victims are especially vulnerable to eating disorders including anorexia nervosa and bulimia, as well as to obesity from overeating. Many say that the act of starving themselves is an attempt to control their own bodies after years of feeling as though their abuser had that control. When a sex abuse victim experiences compulsive overeating, this behavior often stems from a feeling of shame toward his or her body and sexuality. It may also represent a desire to hide his or her body.

OTHER EMOTIONAL AFTEREFFECTS

The following behaviors are common to victims of child physical and sexual abuse or neglect.

- Blocking out some period of early years
- Night terrors
- Self-injuring behaviors (for example, cutting)
- Sexual activity or promiscuity at an early age
- Inappropriate clothing (usually too much clothing for the weather, worn to cover the body)
- Specific to incest: gag reflex, difficulty with water hitting the face and difficulty using public bathrooms

There is worse lasting emotional damage when a child's sexual abuse started before the age of six, and lasted for several years. Among child and teen victims of sexual abuse there is a 42 percent increased chance of suicidal thoughts during adolescence. In the teen years, sex abuse victims show significantly higher rates of illegal drug and alcohol use, prostitution and teen pregnancy.

A FEW WORDS ABOUT
OUR MEMORIES OF CHILD ABUSE

Memories of abuse experienced at a young age are often repressed until they're triggered by an incident in the victim's adult life, or searched for and retrieved through psychotherapy. False memory syndrome is a topic that regularly gets a lot of attention in the media, and it's often overplayed. What's dangerous is when the validity of memories of abuse that come back to victims much later in life are questioned because of some high-profile cases of false or implanted memories. An example is the McMartin Preschool case, in which the reported memories of small children were found to be false; the result of suggestion by therapists assigned to help prosecutors build a case.

Here's what we all have to keep in mind in order to balance these few notorious cases. Of course, some people do misremember events that happened long ago. This is particularly true if there is manipulation by a third party, as in the case of a divorce, when one parent wants to malign the other and tries to implant false memories of sexual abuse in their child, or when a grown child has a preexisting emotional agenda with the accused parent or other perpetrator. So, yes, of course it happens and it's terrible to have someone's reputation ruined by false charges.

But most of the time, recovered memories of abuse are real and credible. Not only that, the vast majority of child sexual abuse cases go unreported. If we put up another roadblock, like blanket questioning of repressed memories, it means fewer victims will come forward. There has to be a middle ground. But if we're going to give the benefit of the doubt to anyone, let's give it to the child, either during or after the abuse experience. Having a qualified therapist help unlock unconscious memories is a vital first step for anyone of any age, so the person abused can begin the process of healing.

HEALING FROM CHILD SEXUAL ABUSE

Therapists who treat adult and child survivors of sexual abuse have identified four steps and stages to healing.

1. After getting safely away from an abuser, it's critically important to obtain treatment for any addiction, mental disorder or other life-threatening condition that's afflicting us as a direct result

of the abuse. In my case, that meant dealing with my anorexia before going too far into the abuse issues.

2. Then we must acknowledge and release the painful memories of abuse. This is so important, and so hard! To accomplish this step, we have to return emotionally to the experience of abuse and realize that we did not "deserve it" and that there is nothing we could have done to stop it or prevent it. That's how we come to understand that it's not our fault. With this step comes the realization that any shame we're feeling is misplaced. It belongs with our abuser. This is also called empowerment: me as a victim taking my power back from the perpetrator.

3. Next, we must challenge any core beliefs or ingrained patterns of thoughts and feelings we've formed as a result of the abuse. Examples are "I am worthless" or "I don't deserve to be loved." In many cases, we also feel the need to mourn the years of childhood we lost to the abuse.

4. Finally, victims need to seek help and support from others. This might be a trained counselor, a member of the clergy or a sympathetic family member or friend. For many abuse victims, Twelve Step programs or other groups specifically for survivors of sexual abuse are valuable for long-term recovery.

For more information, visit the Lauren's Kids Foundation website at www.LaurensKids.org.

APPENDIX B

Ron Book's
Ten Safety Tips for Parents

I'm often asked by parents what I wish I'd known back when we unknowingly brought a sexual predator into our home; or the things I would do differently today if I was hiring a nanny for my children. Here's what I tell them.

1. **Background Checks**

   When you bring someone into your home to care for your kids, you should truly know everything about them. Be aware that simple reference checks, in which you contact people identified as previous employers, can be totally unreliable. Full criminal background checks are helpful, but also not conclusive, due to the vast underreporting of crimes against children. There are also problems with foreign nationals and the databases, or lack thereof, in other countries that might track child molesters.

2. **Cameras**

   Putting surveillance cameras in your home may seem excessive, but remember that 90 percent of child sexual abuse is committed by someone the child knows and trusts. Today, cameras are not only inexpensive, but the technology allows you remote access from your car, hotels (when out of town), etc.

3. **Warning Signs**

    After you have a regular babysitter or a nanny in your home, pay attention to warning signs that something is not right. Some of these are clearer in children over three, and in families with siblings. For example:

    - Favoritism of one child over others
    - Clear signs of inappropriate terms of endearment
    - Check the long list of warning signs in Appendix A: "Facts and Fictions about Child Abuse"

    Make surprise visits to check on how things are going when you're not expected at home.

    If you see any of these warning signs, don't be afraid to be inquisitive and pry. Always talk to your children about daily activities and show interest in their feelings.

4. **Teach your children about their bodies and the difference between appropriate and inappropriate touch.**
    The Lauren's Kids Foundation *It's Okay to Tell* Curriculum offers some basic instruction in this area.

5. **Don't be afraid to investigate suspicions—your child's life may depend on it.**

6. **Teach your children that secrets are always to be shared with you—always.**

7. **Don't ever allow your child, if under the age of thirteen, to be alone in a public place.**

8. Know with whom your child is spending time, and be very careful about allowing your child in out-of-the-way places with other adults or older children.

9. Listen carefully when your child says he has to tell you something, especially when it seems difficult to talk about.

10. Talk to your child about personal space.
    Let children know their bodies belong to them, and that only they can make decisions about what happens to their bodies.

ACKNOWLEDGMENTS

While there is not enough paper in the world to adequately thank everyone who has helped me become the person I am today, please know I appreciate and acknowledge you all each and every day. However, I would like to express my deepest and sincerest gratitude to so many who have enriched my life on a personal level, and also to those who have contributed to Lauren's Kids and helped make us who and what we are today. I would also like to thank those who helped with the task of putting my story to paper.

To Mom, Dad, Samantha, Chase, the Weinroth, Gould and Horden families, Aunt Laverne, Auntie Mame, Uncle Bill, Aunt Rosemary, Grandpa Book, Mariella, Vance and baby Isabella Aloupis, Tara Zuckerman and family, Kristin Cline, Blair Byrnes, the Lim family, Lauren's Kids board of directors, Lisa Ling, Tracy Wilson Mourning, Alonzo Mourning, Lisa Young, Tony Fiorentino, Eric Reid, Charlie and Lisa Fernandes, Dwyane Wade, the Miami Dolphins and their CEO, Mike Dee, Mandy Wells, Nancy Cotterman, Kitty Terry, Jennifer Dritt, Terri Poore, Ron Sachs Communications, Melinda Parker, Randy Perkins, Manny Kadre, Publix Supermarkets, Bill Fauerbach, Kim Jaeger, AAA, Vitas Healthcare Corporation, Jack Galardi, Stuart Miller, Marshall Ames, TNT Fireworks, Tommy Glasgow, Terry Anderson, Dennis Siegal, Broward State Attorney Mike Satz, Broward County sheriffs Al Lamberti and Ken Jenne and the entire staff of the Broward Sheriff's Office.

I would especially like to recognize the members of the Florida legislature, who have listened to my story and ideas over the past ten years and who have stood up against childhood sexual abuse, passing laws and providing funding, as they lead our country in their efforts to protect our children.

Special thanks to Victoria Costello and Nancy Nicholas for their help with the book.